Spiritually Yours

Spiritually Yours

Applying Gospel Principles for Personal Progression

S. Brent Farley

International Standard Book Number
0-88290-192-3

Library of Congress Catalog Card Number
81-82054

Horizon Publishers Catalog & Order Number
1068

Printed and Distributed in the
United States of America
by

Horizon Publishers & Distributors Inc.

---

50 South 500 West
P.O. Box 490
Bountiful, Utah 84010

Dedication

. . . to my wife, Janene, our family,
and all the saints who are striving
to live the gospel.

Acknowledgment

Special appreciation is expressed to my wife Janene for her encouragement in my writing. The personnel of Horizon Publishers are extended a special thanks for their quality efforts in the publishing of this book. The cover photo was graciously provided by my friend and colleague, Robert D. Monson. Many others deserve thanks for making this work possible, including those who gave permission to use quotes, and those whose experiences helped to enrich "Spiritually Yours."

Contents

Preface

The pathway of the saints is different from the world's course. It may be referred to as *strange* and *peculiar;* it is *in the world,* but not *of it.* Those who walk it separate themselves for a higher destiny.

In the premortal existence there was a similar separation: a third part failed to walk the path at all, refusing to apply gospel principles that had the power to exalt them.

Now, the separation continues. The pathway of the saints leads toward the celestial kingdom where the greatest degree of happiness possible awaits those who finish the journey. *Spiritually Yours* describes that pathway and gives practical insights into gospel living.

S. Brent Farley

CHAPTER ONE

Faith: The Spark Of Power

It was one of those school holidays that freed me, as a teacher, for a day with the family. We had planned to visit my parents who lived about a forty-five-minute drive to the south. My wife, Janene, was packing a picnic lunch and our children were just beginning to stir in their beds, soon to wake up. While discussing the coming picnic, we were interrupted by the ringing of the phone. I answered cheerfully; the voice on the other end was not cheerful. It was our high priests group leader, who lived only three houses away.

"Bishop, this is Brother Olson. Can you come up right away? My son has passed away."

"I'm on my way," I responded. After giving him the emergency number and suggesting that he call, I hung up the phone and turned to my wife. "Brother Olson's baby son passed away. Do you mind if we cancel the picnic?"

"Of course not," she responded.

"Will you explain things to the children?" Then I left and hurried up the street to the Olson's home.

Brother Olson met me at the door. As I entered, I saw Sister Olson in the living room, beside herself with grief. He led me up the stairs and into the bedroom of the child. It was obvious at a glance that the child was beyond revival.

"Bishop," said Brother Olson, "can we use the power of the priesthood to call him back to life?"

What can one answer to a question like that? Brother Olson and his family were stalwarts in the gospel, models of faithful Latter-day Saints. We believed that the power of the priesthood was greater than death itself. I had to give an answer.

"I don't know, but I'll ask." I knelt down beside a chair near the crib. Brother Olson left the room to comfort his wife. "Heavenly Father," I began, "this faithful brother has asked me a question as his bishop. I cannot answer regarding life and death, but Thou canst. If it be Thy will to give permission, I know that the power of the priesthood can bring this child back to life. May we give him such a blessing?"

I received a distinct answer. It was "no."

By coincidence or inspiration, Brother Olson entered the room just as I concluded my prayer. Still kneeling, I looked around at him and shook my head "no." He shook his head up and down, indicating that he understood and accepted the decision.

About that time we heard sirens and knew that the paramedics were nearing the home. A minute or two later they were rushing up the stairs and into the bedroom. A quick check and attempt at revival brought the same kind of response from the paramedic that I had given Brother Olson. He shook his head from side to side. There was no hope.

Events seemed to rush by. The child was taken outside to a waiting ambulance. His death was confirmed. After comfort from the officers who had attempted to help, they began to leave as the parents of the Olsons began to arrive. I sensed it was time for me to leave, and told Brother Olson that I would be at home all day if there was anything I could do to help.

The harsh reality and suddenness of the child's death began a chain of events to prepare for the funeral. Arrangements were made, the time set, and I was asked if I would speak. I responded with gratitude. Kneeling at my bedside, I prayed for help and insight sufficient that I might be able to give comfort and hope to the family members at the funeral. I felt strongly the message of Galatians 6:10: "As we have therefore opportunity, let us do good unto all men, especially unto them who are of the household of faith." If anyone deserved special treatment, this faithful family did.

The day of the funeral arrived. I was scheduled to be in a regional conference that morning, but called my stake president and indicated that I would leave after the first hour in order to prepare my thoughts for the conducting of the funeral. He gave permission, and indicated that he would also attend the services.

As I left my meeting that morning, I got into my car and again bowed my head in prayer. "Heavenly Father, please guide me. Teach me so that I might offer comfort and information concerning Brother Olson's son." Then I started the car and began to drive through the countryside. I kept my mind open for inspiration, listening for the promptings of the Spirit.

I pulled off the road under the shade of a hugh, sturdy tree. As I looked at the tree, some thoughts began to form in my mind. Each branch of that tree was a member of the living body, though some branches were hidden from view on the opposite side. I thought how that was like Brother Olson's son. Though he had passed away from our view, he was just on the other side of the family tree, still attached as a member of a living family. His membership had not been severed. I had the feeling that the child would continue as an active member of the family, being near to the parents and living children from time to time, especially in times of important decisions. I took a pen and quickly wrote down the thoughts.

I drove on, taking my time and watching for help in preparing for the funeral sermon. Help came. At another point I pulled off the road and walked over to a little stream. I watched the water running over the pebbles, and thought of the "living waters" of the Savior. I thought how the stream of life continued on beyond the grave, and how Brother Olson's son's life had just moved further from view, rather than terminating.

At the conclusion of my journey, I stopped at the West Jordan Cemetery where the child's body would be buried later that day. I walked over to a fresh mound of earth, the only one in the cemetery. I knew that this was where the grave would be. As I stood in front of the grave, I was alone. No one else was in the cemetery, and I was far enough away from the road that no one could tell what I was doing. I bowed my head again in prayer. "Heavenly Father, I thank Thee for blessing me with this rich insight. Please help me to be humble and worthy enough to present this sermon in such a way as to give great comfort to the parents and relatives of this child. Please give me insight and information concerning him, if it be Thy will." As I prayed, I became aware of the presence of Brother Olson's son. With my head bowed and eyes closed, I did not see him, yet I knew he was there. He stood a little above me in the air, just off to my left and in front of me. He had a radiant personality. His age was not that of a child, but of a young man in his prime, much like the missionaries. He had a clear complexion. I sensed the color of his hair and even the style of the cut—much like the missionaries. He was there for just a few seconds, and then he left. With deep gratitude, I closed my prayer. Now I had the conviction, the testimony, and the information that could give the comfort the parents deserved.

I continued on to the stake center where the services would be held. Arriving early, I again sought the help of the Lord and his Spirit in conducting the services.

As the people entered, the spirit of sorrow and an element of gloom seemed to permeate the atmosphere. Though the hope of the gospel was evident, the weight of sorrow was pronounced. The time for beginning the services arrived and the opening prayer was given. Beginning with that prayer and throughout the services, the gloom seemed to dispel as the Spirit moved the congregation in the realization that the child was very much alive and well. As I shared my experiences of that morning, the testimony of life after death welled up in my heart and was carried in spirit to the hearts of the family and friends. At the conclusion of the services, a spirit of solemn joy in the hope of eternal life had replaced the gloom of despair. The mortal shell of the individual had been left behind, but the individual had moved on. The future resurrection would reunite the mortal and immortal bodies, never again to be separated.

After the services and burial, Sister Olson and her husband expressed gratitude, hope, and testimony concerning their son. Sister Olson said how much she appreciated my experience in sensing the presence of her son, and indicated that she also enjoyed an experience where she had felt his presence during an evening prior to the services.

The family had gathered together in the home. The visiting increased, and Sister Olson felt the desire to step outside into the quiet evening air. She stood up, left the visiting group in the living room, passed through the kitchen and out the sliding glass doors onto the veranda. Closing the doors behind her, she looked out across the darkened field and into the starry skies beyond. With the memory of her son, tears filled her eyes. As she stood there crying, she said that she felt her son stand at her side, put his arm around her, and say: "It's all right, Mother."

The visit was not long, but it was real. He left, and after gaining her composure, she returned inside the house with a new witness and comfort of the reality of the continued life of her son, whose earthly shell only was left behind.

The days passed, and many offered comfort. A special group of people who helped parents whose children had passed away from crib death was amazed at the way the Olsons were able to adjust to the loss and keep a positive atmosphere in their lives. They were exemplary models, so to speak. The members of the group did not understand that it was the power sparked from their faith in the gospel that led to such an adjustment.

How does one develop that kind of faith? Where are the beginnings of faith?

For me, the best explanation lies in the masterful discourse on faith contained in Alma 32. Alma is talking to a group of poor people and has borne testimony of the reality and goodness of God. Then he begins to explain the development of faith to them. ". . . Faith is not to have a perfect knowledge of things; therefore if ye have faith ye hope for things which are not seen, which are true."

And now, behold, I say unto you, and I would that ye should remember, that God is merciful unto all who believe on his name; therefore he desireth, in the first place, that ye should believe, yea, even on his word." (Alma 32:21-22.) Continuing, he explained: "Now, as I said concerning faith—that it was not a perfect knowledge—even so it is with my words. Ye cannot know of their surety at first, unto perfection, any more than faith is a perfect knowledge.

"But behold, if ye will awake and arouse your faculties, even to an experiment upon my words, and exercise a particle of faith, yea, even if ye can no more than desire to believe, let this desire work in you, even until ye believe in a manner that ye can give place for a portion of my words." (Alma 32:26-27.)

It seems that the earliest beginnings of faith stem from a hope, or desire, to believe in something. For example, one hears of the restoration of the gospel and says: "Oh, I hope that is true. It would be wonderful if the Lord did have a true church upon the earth."

Perhaps the desire is in a hope for life after death: "I hope there is an eternity where we can live on in love and peace."

When one has such a hope, the foundation for faith is laid. Alma then compares the word to be tested for its truthfulness to a seed. He says:

"Now, if ye give place, that a seed may be planted in your heart, behold, if it be a true seed, or a good seed, if ye do not cast it out by your unbelief, that ye will resist the Spirit of the Lord, behold, it will begin to swell within your breasts; and when you feel these swelling motions, ye will begin to say within yourselves—It must needs be that this is a good seed, or that the word is good, for it beginneth to enlarge my soul; yea, it beginneth to enlighten my understanding, yea, it beginneth to be delicious to me." (Alma 32:28.)

One might hear of the restoration of the gospel and express a hope that such a message is true. If he gives place for that message and allows the spirit of the Lord to work in him, it will bring noticeable results. If, on the other hand, he slams the door in the face of the missionaries, or listens to a rumor that the Mormons could not be the Lord's people and refuses to listen further, he will cast the seed out of his heart and thus will not experience the growth that could otherwise have come.

If he avoids such rash decisions and takes the time to plant the seed, opening himself to the possibility of inspiration from heaven, studying the word and gaining information and evidence concerning its truthfulness, he will begin to have good feelings inside about the question being studied. These feelings will be real—described as a swelling motion, or fullness of heart, in which the sensitivity of the soul is awakened and the thoughts of the mind become clearer. Then Alma said: "Now behold, would not this increase your faith? I say unto you, Yea; nevertheless it hath not grown up to a perfect knowledge." (Alma 32:29.)

That perfect knowledge can come, however, for Alma explains that ". . . As the seed swelleth, and sprouteth, and beginneth to grow, then you must needs say that the seed is good; for behold it swelleth, and sprouteth, and beginneth to grow.

"And now, behold, are ye sure that this is a good seed? I say unto you, Yea; for every seed bringeth forth unto its own likeness." (Alma 32:30-31.)

These good feelings and thoughts will continue to strengthen and build upon one another until one is sure that the seed is good. When the witness of the spirit deepens, a testimony is born. Alma states:

"And now, behold, is your knowledge perfect? Yea, your knowledge is perfect in that thing, and your faith is dormant, and this because ye know, for ye know that the word hath swelled your souls, and ye also know that it hath sprouted up . . ." (Alma 32:34.)

When we moved as a family to California, we purchased a home that had an awful-looking back yard. Weeds were rampant, and the look was undesirable. We had a hope inside that we could change that appearance. Building upon that hope, we began to chop out the weeds and clear the ground for planting. We rototilled, leveled, and worked fertilizer into the soil. Then I went to the local nursery and described the kind of grass I wanted in my back yard. The nurseryman handed me a package of grass seed and said, "This is what you want."

I looked at the picture of grass on the front of the package and accepted his word that my yard could look like that.

When we opened the package of seeds, it did not, of course, look anything like the green picture on the front. Only dry, dead-looking seeds were inside. Nevertheless, we built upon our hope and faith by giving a place for the seeds—planting and watering them.

I watered that brown soil for some time, not knowing that the seeds were softening, swelling, and sprouting in the soil beyond my view. (So it is with faith: it seems to take root and begin its growth, unperceived by others in its early stages.)

One day, while watering, I dropped a coin. Stooping down to retrieve it, my line of sight chanced across a little pocket in the soil and I thought I saw a faint haze of green. Moving closer to the pocket and lying down on the ground, I beheld tiny green shoots beginning to rise from the dirt. I excitedly jumped up and yelled to my wife, "Janene, come quick! The lawn is coming up."

She rushed out of the house and said, "Where? I don't see anything."

"Get down right here and look at that little pocket from this angle."

She did, and saw the haze.

In the next day or two, green blades popped up all over the back yard until there was a consistent haze across the yard. Our hope and faith now became knowledge, and we knew that the seeds we had planted were good.

So it is with the seeds of faith. When they begin to produce, having been properly planted and nourished, one knows with a certainty of their goodness. But Alma warned ". . . after ye have tasted this light is your knowledge perfect?"

"Behold I say unto you, Nay; neither must ye lay aside your faith, for ye have only exercised your faith to plant the seed that ye might try the experiment to know if the seed was good." (Alma 32:35-36.)

If, after our lawn came up, we said, "We've got it made; let's take a vacation," and we left for a month, making no provisions for the watering and care of our lawn, we would return to find the same brown dirt in our back yard that we had prior to the planting. It would not be because the seed was bad, but because we did not nourish the young blades of grass properly.

Some members of the church gain testimonies of its truthfulness, then fail to nourish that testimony. The result is that the testimony dies out and they become inactive. It is not because the church is not true, or the spiritual witness was not real, but because they assumed they could stop caring for the word once it had sprouted. They didn't realize that a testimony can grow and expand with care, but will wither and die without it.

In verses 37 through 42, the seed has become a tree. Even at this stage, Alma warns that lack of care and nourishment will result in withering roots and the death of the tree. If, however, a testimony is nourished, faith continues to increase with knowledge, and the tree begins to produce fruit. What was once a seed nourished and kept alive by the planter now provides nourishment and life for the one who originally cared for it.

It is this fruit from the tree of knowledge and faith that sustained and nourished the Olson family in the loss of their baby son. What had been nourished for years through gospel living now fed them in their hour of trial and need. Their faith became the spark of power.

The fruits of faith thus give strength and beauty to the lives of faithful Latter-day Saints. The end result of such fruit is the partaking of the joys of eternity: ". . . Behold it shall be a tree springing up unto everlasting life."

"And because of your diligence and your faith and your patience with the word in nourishing it, that it may take root in you, behold, by and by ye shall pluck the fruit thereof, which is most precious, which is sweet above all that is sweet, and which is white above all that is white, yea, and pure above all that is pure; and ye shall feast upon this fruit even until ye are filled, that ye hunger not, neither shall ye thirst."

"Then, my brethren, ye shall reap the rewards of your faith, and your diligence, and patience, and long-suffering, waiting for the tree to bring forth fruit unto you." (Alma 32:41-43.)

And the Olsons will again embrace their son in the realms of eternity.

CHAPTER TWO

A Testimony
Of The Prophets

"Would you please clear an aisle," a security guard called through the crowd following the morning session of General Conference. I was standing in a narrow hallway, with other members of the Mormon Tabernacle Choir who were putting their music folders away. As the men ceased visiting and backed up against the music cupboards, I looked to see who or what might be approaching. Expecting to see someone being pushed in a wheel chair, or perhaps a tabernacle official, I was startled to recognize someone coming whose presence fulfilled a desire that I had hardly dared to dream.

As a boy I had listened to members bearing their testimonies of the gospel. "I know that The Church of Jesus Christ of Latter-day Saints is true," they would state. "I know that Joseph Smith was a prophet." I wondered about those statements. Particularly did I wonder *how* they could know that Joseph Smith was a prophet. He had been dead years before they were born. How could they know if they never knew him personally?

I found out how they knew one day as I was startled in another little hallway in the basement of our home. Clutching a Book of Mormon in my hands, I knelt and prayed to Heavenly Father, expressing a desire to know the truth. When I left that little enclosure, my mind had opened with a communication of the Spirit. I had been caught by surprise, not really having anticipated what occurred. I knew then what Moroni meant when he said, ". . . He will manifest the truth of it unto you, by the power of the Holy Ghost." (Moroni 10:4.) I had never met the Prophet Joseph Smith, but the Spirit of the Holy Ghost bridged the gap. Now I had a testimony of a prophet. I really knew.

Not long after that experience it occurred to me that I knew Joseph Smith was a prophet, but what about the current prophet, who at that time was David O. McKay? Not knowing any better method of finding out, I knelt one evening in the course of my regular prayers and simply asked Heavenly Father, "Is David O. McKay Thy prophet?"

The witness was not as burning as the first experience, but the feeling was unmistakable. I knew that David O. McKay was the Lord's chosen servant.

Joseph Fielding Smith came next and I did not feel it was appropriate to ask again. I knew the Lord would correctly place one of His sons at the head of the church; I had received sufficient witnesses.

In times to follow, I only faltered once in the desire to ask again, and that came when I learned of my first opportunity to be in the same room with a prophet of the Lord. This occurred in a college ward in Tempe, Arizona. It was announced that Harold B. Lee, President of the Church, would speak to a special gathering of college students. I received an admittance pass for Janene (my wife) and I to attend the meeting.

As the day of his visit approached, I wondered if I might ask for another witness regarding this special position of prophet. I wondered and debated, thinking on one hand that I need not ask each time a prophet was chosen, but on the other that this was a special situation. I would see the prophet in person, even if from a distance.

The day of special importance arrived, and my wife and I were seated about twenty rows from the stand where the prophet would sit. I wondered what would happen when he entered the room, and which side would he enter from? While wondering, the audience rose almost as if on cue, and I knew the prophet had entered the room. "We thank thee, O God, for a prophet . . ." The words of the hymn came spontaneously from the lips of the members. I strained and squinted for a glimpse of the man, but could not get a clear view until he was seated before us. "Dare I ask for a witness?" I wondered. "Would I be worthy if I did? Would it show a lack of faith because I had received prior testimony of other prophets? If I was qualified and it was right, would I lose the opportunity simply because I had paused to debate with myself?" The reasoning became almost silly, and I concluded to forget the whole matter and concentrate on the message of President Lee. He was now speaking. I listened intently, trying to understand his message and analyze its potential for application in my life. I completely forgot about the question of receiving a witness.

President Lee concluded with his testimony. Closing remarks and a benediction ended the meeting. I thought the highlight of the day had passed, but it was just now approaching. As the prophet and his little group left the stand for the exit, I saw them turn toward the exit opposite their entering point. I suddenly became excited, for this meant that the prophet would pass on my side of the congregation, and I would get a twenty- to thirty-foot glimpse of the president of the church; the closest glimpse of my life. I watched through the open isle between our row of chairs and the row in front of us for him to pass. Not being able to see clearly for the people standing in front of me, I watched intently to the side for those brief seconds in which he would cross my line of sight.

As soon as he entered the clearing between rows, something literally breathtaking happened. Upon his appearance, I received the most powerful witness from the Lord that I had ever received in my life to that point. It felt to me as though a spiritual sword had been thrust through my soul. It was a piercing witness of concentrated power, sufficient to cause me to gasp in response. Tears burst into my eyes. My reaction was audible to Janene, who turned and asked, "What's the matter?"

Being choked with emotion, I said in words broken by feelings, "I'll tell you later."

It was about a half hour later, while driving home, that I gained enough control of my emotions that I could share the experience. I had received far more than I had debated asking for; so much more that I knew I need never question the inspired calling of the prophet at the head of the church.

Spencer W. Kimball was the next prophet. I didn't need to ask. The desire never crossed my mind. I already knew from prior experience that this was the man of God. What to my surprise, when the aisle was opened at the request of the security guard in the Tabernacle on Temple Square, to look out and to see the prophet of the Lord coming directly toward us. As he approached, he held out his hand to greet the men of the choir by whom he would pass. I was just a little ways down the line. As he neared me, shaking hands with each individual, he looked at the brother across the aisle and took his hand. Fearing that the opportunity to shake hands with the prophet would pass, I held out my right hand in such a manner that it would brush the prophet's coat, and he would know there was another individual not wanting to be missed. As soon as my hand touched his sleeve, without looking around, he slipped his left hand up and into my right, then held on with a tightness that assured me I would not be overlooked. As soon as he finished his greeting to the gentleman opposite me, he turned and smiled. There I stood, holding hands with the prophet of the Lord, who was only inches away.

I had read stories about individuals who had visited personally with a prophet. They described how they felt when he gazed into their eyes, as if to read the lines in the innermost depths of their souls. But my experience was not the same. I gazed deep into the eyes of the prophet. They were clear, bright, radiant and youthful, vibrant with love and a clarity of purpose. I was enthralled.

Our encounter was only for a few seconds. I am sure he said something to me, but it must not have registered. I don't recall a single word of his greeting. But I'll never forget the bond of love I sensed as I gazed into his eyes. This was indeed the prophet of the Lord, and I gazed for a moment into his soul.

A few weeks after that marvelous experience, I learned a lesson worthy of being categorized as a "pearl of great price." Janene and I had just returned from a Tabernacle Choir rehearsal. We were tired. After evening prayers, we turned out the lights and retired. Sleep was just approaching when the phone rang. I answered and was greeted by the voice of a councilor in the stake presidency. After an unusual greeting for that time of the night, he asked if Janene and I could come down to the stake president's office for a visit. I said yes, and reached for my appointment book, while asking, "When would you like us to come down?"

"Can you come right now?" he asked.

I looked at the clock: 10:30 p.m. "Well, we're not dressed for an appointment with the stake president, but if you'll give us a few minutes, we can be there."

At 10:45 p.m., we drove into the church parking lot and parked near the only lighted window of the building. A few minutes later we were seated in front of the desk of the stake president, chatting casually with him and his two counselors.

At about 11:15 p.m., the president said, "Well, I guess you're wondering why we called you down here this time of the night." (My wife had suggested along the way that we might be called as stake dance directors, a hope she had always harbored and I had always feared.) I nodded positively. Then he said it. "Brother Farley, President Kimball wants you to be the new bishop of the West Jordan 18th Ward."

With that statement, I looked almost in reflex at the picture of President Kimball that hung on the wall behind him. It was as if the face in the picture came alive. A message of "That's right" passed from the portrait to me. How it happened, I couldn't explain, but I knew the look of the prophet's eyes, and I felt the confirming message. Then the picture became only an image again. There was nothing for me to say or question. I loved the prophet, and I realized that he was interested in my service, even though he was not present during the call, and perhaps not even aware at the time. I accepted, and left the office at about 11:30 p.m. to contemplate a new era of service.

Perhaps a fitting summary for these experiences came in Laguna Beach, California, as I stood in what once was a church-owned home overlooking the ocean. Following the sale of the home, I was asked by Elder Ferren L. Christensen, Regional Representative of the Twelve, if I would assist in moving the pieces of furniture from the home. We were to begin in the

bedroom. As we reached to remove the bedspread, the first step in dis-
mantling the bed for removal, Elder Christensen stopped us.

"Before you take this bed apart," he said, "I want to tell you some-
thing. Five prophets of the Lord have slept in this room: George Albert
Smith, David O. McKay, Joseph Fielding Smith, Harold B. Lee, and
Spencer W. Kimball."

I was standing in work clothes, mentally set for the labor of the afternoon. But for a moment I could have been in a temple. The purifying fire
of the Spirit filled my soul as I listened to Elder Christensen's words. I
knew for myself that this room had held the servants of the Lord. Again,
I was enhanced in my testimony of the prophets of the Lord. I knew. I really
knew. I had received another witness.

CHAPTER THREE

The Wealth Within The Scriptures

Many of the touching moments of my life have come while studying the scriptures. Answers to prayers, feelings of closeness to prophets of other eras, insights into theology, and answers to life's problems have been given from the printed page, enlivened by the Spirit of the Lord.

I've found that the voice of the Lord is as close as my standard works.

"These words are not of men nor of man, but of me; wherefore, you shall testify they are of me and not of man;

"For it is my voice which speaketh them unto you; for they are given by my Spirit unto you, and by my power you can read them one to another; and save it were by my power you could not have them;

"Wherefore, you can testify that you have heard my voice, and know my words." (D&C 18:34-36.)

A daily reception of the voice of the Lord can be gained by daily involvement with the scriptures. The investment of fifteen to thirty minutes per day, consistently spent in reading the scriptures, can bring marvelous returns in knowledge, understanding, faith, hope, security, and spirituality.

The key to expertise involves commitment, action, and consistency. When one has decided to regularly study the scriptures and commits to do so, a giant step has been taken. (Many saints fail in scripture study because they never start mentally.) After committing to read daily, the action of reading must follow, because faith without works is dead. (James 2:20.) Once the reading is begun, consistency of study is necessary to maintain the thrust of commitment.

Here are ten tips for getting the most from your scripture study once you have started the rolling wheel of commitment, action, and consistency.

1. Make a blueprint for studying the scriptures. If one has never read the standard works, this involves a decision as to where to start. Select the standard work most interesting to you. Then arrange a reading order that will include all of the standard works.

Generally, read straight through the book. If you bog down in a certain area the first time through, consider skipping over that section and continuing when the reading becomes more interesting and understandable. Genealogies, old rites and rituals, and sometimes passages especially hard to understand the first time through can have the effect of "bogging one down" until discouragement and lack of interest begin to widen the gap between commitment and action in scripture study. Skip the "marshy" areas the first time through. Come back to them later when a better foundation of gospel knowledge can help clear up the "muddy" spots and add insight and interest to previously difficult passages.

Drink more from the pure waters than the diluted. In other words, place more emphasis upon the standard works than upon commentaries. The standard works represent the words of the Lord; commentaries represent the words of others concerning the words of the Lord. Commentaries are helpful, but not as authoritative or inspiring as the scriptures themselves.

Select a regular time for reading the scriptures. It would be helpful if this time were consistent each day. Ideally this would be during a quiet time of the day, perhaps early in the morning or later in the evening. Early morning tends toward sharpness of mind, evening toward reflective and contemplative ability. Both are good. The time that is available daily is most important; if there is a choice between alternatives, then one should select the time most conducive to personal sharpness and learning ability. If there is no time available, make some. It's that important!

2. Get mentally set before reading. A priesthood manual counseled: "The ability to read and enjoy the scriptures requires preparation, prayer, and reverence whereas anyone can pick up a news magazine and begin to read and understand it without the slightest effort at preparation. The next time you have a few moments to read, purposefully pick up your scriptures. Then pray, seek for the Spirit of God to guide you in your reading, and you will begin to get more from your scripture study."*

Peter said that ". . . Prophecy came not in old time by the will of man: but holy men of God spake as they were moved by the Holy Ghost." (2 Peter 1:21.) Since the scriptures were given by inspiration, they can only be properly understood by inspiration. A petition to the Lord for help in understanding

---

*When Thou Art Converted Strengthen Thy Brethren, 1974-75 Priesthood Study Guide, p. 31.

should precede every reading period. Even the shortest of reading periods are more meaningful and valuable if prefaced by prayer. Then, as you read, the same thing that happened to Lehi may happen to you: "And it came to pass that as he read, he was filled with the Spirit of the Lord." (1 Nephi 1:12.)

3. Don't worry so much about lower-level facts; concentrate on higher-level concepts. It's nice to remember who said what, where and when, but facts do not have the saving power that concepts do. Look for the meanings in the scriptures pertinent to you, the principles involved in the passages you are reading. What brought happiness and misery, success and failure? How did the scriptural characters deal with conflicts, temptation, discouragement, and success? What attitudes and abilities made Nephi different from Laman? When were the people happiest? Why? What led to that condition? How does Satan work among individuals? How does the strength of the Lord affect the affairs of men? What is the purpose of living the gospel? How can I qualify to feel the joy of this or that great individual?

Answers to these and similar questions are far more valuable than being able to say who said what, in which set of records, between what events.

4. Mark your scriptures by underlining or coloring in the parts that are meaningful or beautiful to you. This personalizes your set of scriptures and highlights those passages that touch you in some way. This may be valuable to your children as they skim over your standard works and note what impressed you, too. It also makes it a little easier to return to a favorite passage. Sometimes when you have only a few minutes for reading, you might just read some of the colored-in passages, knowing that they were selected because of their power and beauty to you.

Some years ago, I felt I had reached a plateau in my spiritual development and had difficulty getting off of it. I was "spinning my wheels," seemingly getting nowhere in my progress. I was looking for insight and comfort, a clue to help me overcome the obstacle before me. One day after returning from work, I sat at our living room table and took out my scriptures. I prayed that the Lord would guide me in my search for help, then decided to read some of the underlined passages in my triple combination. I turned at random and began reading, changed my mind, and selected another set of marked passages. After a few seconds, I thumbed through the pages to a different section and began reading an area I had previously marked with red pencil. There was the answer for which I had been seeking, already underlined. It was exactly for me, or so it seemed, for the passage was tailored to my need. After reading, I knew I had been directed to that section, for I gained the insight and strength that helped me break down the obstacle to my personal growth. Had the passage not been marked in red, it would have been less likely that I would have found it so readily.

5. If you only have a few minutes a day to read, write down questions you come up with for further research outside of your daily time block for scripture reading. Later on you can come back to the questions raised from your prior reading. You may decide to research the question, table it indefinitely, or drop it if it doesn't seem that important to you the second time around. This will help keep tangents from slowing or stopping your progress through the standard works.

You might want to save your list of questions and then get together with someone else for a discussion period that could prove exciting.

The very fact that you wrote a question down will aid in remembering it. It may be answered as you listen to a lesson in Sunday school, a talk in sacrament meeting, or a lecture during education week.

6. Write down specific insights in a journal. Your reading will produce feelings and knowledge that are worth recording. As you do so, your reading experience with the scriptures will be much more valuable. This also helps in the task of keeping a personal journal and preserves for your posterity some of the reactions you had to the scriptures. By reviewing your journal occasionally, you will strengthen your gospel knowledge and begin to perceive patterns within the scriptures that will aid you in your own life. There seems to be something magical in the process of writing down insights and feelings that puts a zest and special memory into your scripture study. If you record your feelings aided by the power of the Holy Ghost, you may even produce a personal set of records that could serve with scripture-like power for your loved ones.

7. Use cross references, topical guides, footnotes, maps, and other study aids contained within your scriptures when appropriate for further clarification or research. It would pay you to spend some time just experimenting with the various aids available until you know how to use them. Ask someone to help you when you get stumped. Solving the problem will make you more comfortable with your standard works and give you a valuable study skill.

8. Ponder. Next to preliminary prayer and then scripture reading, this is perhaps the most important aspect of studying. During your reading, new insights will begin to form. Pause awhile to think about these insights and relate them to what you already know. Be open in thought so that the Lord can put ideas into your mind; be receptive in attitude so that the Lord can touch your heart with the feelings of the spirit.

"Yea, behold, I will tell you in your mind and in your heart, by the Holy Ghost, which shall come upon you and which shall dwell in your heart.

"Now, behold, this is the spirit of revelation . . ." (D&C 8:2-3.)

After reading, pause a few moments for reflection. Leave the mind open and free from the cares of the day. This has the effect of tuning in your mind to the right channel, like turning the dial on a radio until the station comes in the clearest.

I've attempted to define "pondering" in poetic form:

> Pondering: stillness embued with thoughts
> Clothed in the feelings of prayer,
> Knowing God is near.
>
> The senses, temple-like in awe,
> Turn upward in anticipation
> Of celestial reception.
>
> A time when heart and mind
> Are bonded, seeking in unity
> Communion with divinity.

Throughout the day, think about what you read. This solidifies gospel concepts and helps to develop a clean mind, thus aiding in qualifying for the confidence spoken of in the Doctrine and Covenants: ". . .Let virtue garnish thy thoughts unceasingly; then shall thy confidence wax strong in the presence of God. . . ." (D&C 121:45.)

9. Make application of your reading to your own life. Look for ways to apply your knowledge and become a better person. Make application to your family so their lives can be improved. Relate the teachings of the scriptures to the world in which you live.

As you attend gospel-oriented classes, relate your knowledge to the subject being studied.

Follow the example of a Nephite prophet who did the same thing: ". . . For I did liken all scriptures unto us, that it might be for our profit and learning." (1 Nephi 19:23.)

Perhaps you are reading in the Book of Mormon:

"Yea, come unto Christ, and be perfected in him, and deny yourselves of all ungodliness; and if ye shall deny yourselves of all ungodliness and love God with all your might, mind and strength, then is his grace sufficient for you, that by his grace ye may be perfect in Christ; and if by the grace of God ye are perfect in Christ, ye can in nowise deny the power of God." (Moroni 10:32.)

You pause to think about what you have just read. You have been having difficulty in overcoming a particular temptation. Because it seems attractive, you have felt guilty even at the thoughts of being tempted, even though you have not fallen to the act or allowed the thought to linger. Yet, it recurs, and you feel frustrated because of it. It is discouraging because you are sometimes attracted toward something not in harmony with the gospel. You have often wondered how you could be victorious and avoid even the thoughts of the temptation.

You review the scripture again, sensing that the key to your success is there. The scripture says to come to Christ, which is what you want to do. It talks of being perfect in him, a goal you seek but that seems illusive in reality. How can you get from the temptation to the security of the Lord?

The scripture said to deny yourself of all ungodliness. The temptation you've had fits within that category. You thought you had failed when the temptation seemed attractive, that the battle was lost for the day. You should have been repulsed, you think. But a thought crosses your mind. Why would the scripture say "deny yourself?" If temptations were not presented in an attractive manner, one would have no problem resisting. But if it appeared attractive, then the way to resist would require a denial. The denial is not a failure, but a success. You think of an example to illustrate the concept you are gaining.

If I were overweight and wanted to lose, I would have to cut down on my eating. It is likely that after I made the decision to eat less, food would appear even more attractive. Yet, if I gave in, I wouldn't lose weight. The next time I see a piece of pie or cake, I will have to say honestly: "Even though that food looks attractive, I know it is not good for me. Therefore, I am going to deny myself, resist the pull, and gain the victory. I know if I do so, I will attain the physical proportions I seek. My desire to achieve better weight proportions is stronger than my desire for the food."

You decide to make a resolution. The next time that temptation comes, I will expect it to appear attractive. But the fact that it appears attractive is not the decisive factor in the struggle; I will say to myself that even though it seems attractive, I will deny myself as the scripture counsels, knowing it will not be good for me. Then I will take the next step and emphasize my love of God with all my strength. I will center my thoughts and feelings upon Him. If I do that, then through the grace of God I will gain the strength to overcome that weakness and the time will come when the temptation will not appear attractive to me any more. Then I will be perfect in that thing, because of the power of God helping me after I deny myself and turn to Him.

10. Talk about your reading. One of the signs indicating that one places value upon something is if one talks about it. Family home evenings provide excellent times for discussing principles of the scriptures. The discussion will clarify and solidify your concepts and feelings. Private conversations with friends or family members of similar belief provide another opportunity for expression.

Perhaps a family devotional in the morning before everyone leaves for daily tasks would be helpful. Here each member could take a turn presenting an idea gained from scripture reading. The scripture could be read aloud to the family, then a selected individual could begin by sharing feelings and thoughts about that scripture, its meaning, value, and application.

There will be special teaching moments with children that will come along unexpectedly. These moments are especially powerful if the parent can draw from scripture reading a thought that applies to the situation.

One of my daughters was feeling a loss of self-worth when my wife entered the room, sensed the situation, and drew from the concept in D&C 18:10: "Remember the worth of souls is great in the sight of God . . ." Paraphrasing the Savior's thoughts and making personal application by example and testimony, my wife administered effective medicine for the ailment.

When the husband and wife can take a few moments occasionally to talk about the scriptures, a special set of moments will glow with the brightness of the gospel as a love for one another and God deepens.

Talking about the scriptures is important. The whole concept of missionary work centers around that principle.

Those ten tips can make the scriptures "live."

One other point should be mentioned regarding scripture study. The conference talks and statements from the living prophet constitute scripture as important as the standard works. These writings should be studied in the same way as the other scriptures.

The Lord has left His will for us to read and study; it is found within the scriptures, and is available to every Latter-day Saint. It is a wonderful inheritance.

CHAPTER FOUR

Turning Trials Into Triumphs

"Bishop, have you experienced many trials in your life?"

The question from the class instructor caught him a little off guard, but his response came rather easily: "The wind of trials has never ceased to blow."

"What do you do, then?"

"Lean into the wind and keep walking."

That response stayed with me long after the class had ended. Certainly I had not faced the trials that many others had, and certainly none such as the prophets and apostles endured; yet I sensed their consistent pressure. Why was that so? What was the purpose of trials? Was I failing or succeeding when they came?

With time and study, I came to view trials, not so much as negative hardships to endure, but rather, as positive challenges capable of producing growth and happiness.

Lehi said in the Book of Mormon, "For it must needs be, that there is an opposition in all things. If not so, . . . righteousness could not be brought to pass, neither wickedness, neither holiness nor misery, neither good nor bad . . . no life neither death, . . . happiness nor misery, neither sense nor insensibility." (2 Nephi 2:11.)

I certainly wanted to attain happiness and holiness, which could not come without opposition, so trials could apparently serve as stepping stones rather than stumbling blocks. The Lord had said, "My people must be tried in all things, that they may be prepared to receive the glory that I have for them . . ." (D&C 136:31.) Remove the trials and remove the glory. They were necessary. But how many trials? Could they be lessened? Was life to be difficult and bruising, or could the fruits of joy and peace be gathered along the way? I found that the answers largely depended upon me.

As a part of the test of mortality (see Abraham 3:25) trials are approved experiences for our lives. We cannot dismiss them. In fact, Brigham Young said:

"Every trial and experience you have passed through is necessary for your salvation . . . Every vicissitude we pass through is necessary for experience and example, and for preparation to enjoy that reward which is for the faithful . . .''*

The conclusion? We must learn to deal with trials so that we may prove ourselves of sufficient quality to merit eternal joy. Progress toward that goal brings stability and satisfaction to life.

What are the alternatives when faced with a trial?

Sometimes, in my service as a bishop, I would find a distraught ward member pouring out his or her troubles, painting such a gloomy picture that it seemed life was at the bottom of the pit. If I knew the member was a stable Latter-day Saint, I would sometimes suggest the least attractive alternative in dealing with the trial, knowing that such a suggestion would cause a "U turn" in the road of gloom and point out a brighter destination than had been pictured during the conference. "Well," I would respond, "you could give up and run away."

After an immediate but quiet response of shock, the member would come back, "Oh, no, I could never do that! I really do love my family in spite of the troubles."

The turn had been made, and we would look at another alternative: how then can we deal with the trials and turn them into triumphs?

In working on such an objective, it helps if one has a concept of some possible sources of trials. Understanding a beginning can often aid in determining the end. Following are some of the possible sources of trials, with suggestions to aid in turning them into triumphs.

1. One source of trials could be God's testing. Take the example of Job. Perhaps one of his missions in life was to leave a perfect model of dealing with trials of this source. Through a gloom so terrible that he said, ". . . I am escaped with the skin of my teeth . . ." (Job 19:20), endured a stalwart with a testimony so bright that he wished it was ". . . graven with an iron pen and lead in the rock for ever!"

"For I know that my redeemer liveth, and that he shall stand at the latter day upon the earth:

---

*Priesthood Manual, 1977-78, p. 134.

"And though after my skin worms destroy this body, yet in my flesh shall I see God." (Job 19:24-26.)

It is fun, when reading the scriptures, to thumb ahead and see how things turn out. Sometimes in our lives, when difficult times are upon us, we wish we could thumb a few pages ahead and see what happens. We cannot do that with our lives, but we can with Job's. The end result of his encounter with trials was that ". . . the Lord turned the captivity of Job, . . ." and ". . . blessed the latter end of Job more than his beginning." (Job 42:10, 12.)

What is the prescription for dealing with trials that we gain from Job's example? Don't lose your testimony! No matter what happens, hang on to that testimony! Then put things in perspective, as viewed through the lens of experience with Job, and have faith that the end result can be better than the state before the trial. As Paul said, "We know that all things work together for good to them that love God . . ." (Romans 8:28.) With such a perspective, courage begins to well up, and the challenge of defeat begins to shrink, as the strength of righteous endurance expands.

Abraham provided another example in this realm of trial (see Genesis 22.) The Lord said: "Abraham was commanded to offer his son Isaac; nevertheless, it was written: Thou shalt not kill. Abraham, however, did not refuse, and it was accounted unto him for righteousness." (D&C 132:36.)

What principle was demonstrated? Unquestioning obedience. Abraham was ready to obey the Lord, even though the trial did not seem justifiable, or even logical.

I appreciate to a small degree how Abraham must have felt in determining to give up his only son. My wife and I had been married less than two years when I had to face a situation that brought deeper empathy for Abraham's decision. I awakened one evening and felt a "heaviness" in the room. It was as if the molecules of air were weights pressing upon me. It was somber, sullen, dark. I had the clear and distinct impression that my wife lay at the point of death (though there had been nothing wrong with her previously), and the voice of the Lord came into my mind, asking, "Will you give her to me?" (It was not an audible voice, but a sentence that passed through my mind.)

I was fully awake; it was not a dream, but a real experience. The impressions were clear and unmistakable.

I don't know why I answered as I did, nor why the response came so quickly. Perhaps it was the story of Abraham that had made a mark upon my memory; perhaps it was my mission, or my temple covenants. Perhaps it was the promptings of the Spirit that preceded the hesitancy of logic. At any rate, my mental response was "Yes Lord: if you want her, she's yours."

In the next moment or two, thoughts of sorrow and anxiety flooded down upon me as though the waters of a dam had broken through. How could I exist without her? What would I say when I phoned my parents? How could I explain things to a little girl in the next room who wasn't old enough to speak? Would life hold any hope for our small family?

The sorrow never materialized, for shortly after my reply to the Lord the heavy atmosphere in the room suddenly became light and peaceful. With the change, I knew that my wife would not pass away. So great was the feeling of peace that I slipped quickly back into a restful sleep for the remainder of the night. When I awakened, however, the experience was bright upon my memory, and my feelings were so poignant that I was unable to share them with my wife for some time.

When I arose, I thought: "Oh, Abraham, I appreciate how you must have felt." And I appreciated his example.

2. Another source of trial comes from giving in to the temptations of Satan, ". . . for Satan is abroad in the land, and he goeth forth deceiving the nations." (D&C 52:14.) When an individual invests in a brightly colored package of sin, the chains of hell are quietly prepared while the facade continues. The resultant loss of spirituality and freedom materializes into a trial of failure and unhappiness. As Alma said, " . . . Wickedness never was happiness." (Alma 41:10.) As the poet describes it:

Showy Gifts

It's wrapped in cheerful colors,
Highlighted by a bow;
The contents are a secret
The viewers do not know.

It's advertised so highly,
With promises of glee
For each and every purchaser
Who opens secretly.

Onlookers view with envy
As buyers pass them by,
Gripping showy boxes,
With expectations high.

The show is superficial,
The package holds no prize;
The outward beauty vanishes
To unsupported lies.

And so the gifts from Satan,
(Emptiness within)
Consist of sets of packages
In showy lure of sin.

Trials within this area (giving in to temptation) can be solved by repentance and future resistance to temptation.

Some individuals claim that having been on the "opposite side of the fence" from righteousness, and then being converted, makes them better members of the church, because they have seen both sides. If that were the best manner of saintly preparation, the Savior would have committed sins, then repented and said "Follow me." So that there would be no question as to the best route in time or eternity, He did not do that. His personal example showed the best manner of dealing with temptations: He overcame all of them and lived a perfect, sinless life. "Therefore I would that ye should be perfect even as I, or your Father who is in heaven is perfect." (3 Nephi 12:48.)

The best path to tread is one that never yields to temptation or sin. The best of mortals will come the closest to His record, and any deviance will be best rectified by early and sincere repentance.

"But the devil made me do it," say some.

Not so, say the scriptures.

Every temptation of Satan is countered with a promise from God: "There hath no temptation taken you but such as is common to man: but God is faithful, who will not suffer you to be tempted above that ye are able; but will with the temptation also make a way to escape, that ye may be able to bear it." (1 Corinthians 10:13.)

A good motto is: temptations were made to be overcome.

3. Another source of trials stems from the normal use of free agency in making decisions between alternatives. The Lord expects us to reach conclusions, often on our own.

"For behold, it is not meet that I should command in all things; for he that is compelled in all things, the same is a slothful and not a wise servant; wherefore he receiveth no reward.

"Verily I say, men should be anxiously engaged in a good cause, and do many things of their own free will, and bring to pass much righteousness;

"For the power is in them, wherein they are agents unto themselves." (D&C 58:26-28.)

The trials of daily decisions require personal effort in helping to produce a solution. Two scriptures offer counsel that is especially helpful in this area.

"Behold, you have not understood; you have supposed that I would give it unto you, when you took no thought save it was to ask me.

"But, behold, I say unto you, that you must study it out in your mind; then you must ask me if it be right, and if it is right I will cause that your bosom shall burn within you; therefore, you shall feel that it is right.

"But if it be not right you shall have no such feelings, but you shall have a stupor of thought that shall cause you to forget the thing which is wrong; therefore, you cannot write that which is sacred save it be given you from me." (D&C 9:7-9.)

Although this was given specifically to Oliver Cowdery after his failing to be able to translate, it is a method sometimes recurring in the lives of saints as they seek guidance from the Lord. After studying the alternatives, reasoning out the possibilities, seeking counsel, and evaluating feelings, a decision can be reached and presented to the Lord for verification. If it is verified, a warm or glowing feeling produced by the Holy Ghost will occur within one's breast. If the decision is not correct, no such sensation will come; rather, the thoughts will not seem to fit together as well. The logic will not be sensed, portions may be forgotten, and it may seem "cloudy" within the mind. This indicates that the decision is not correct and must be reworked.

This method of verification is a gift of the Spirit, available to the saints as the Lord wills. It will not occur every time verification is sought, but it is one valid method that saints should be prepared to receive.

The other scripture that is especially helpful is very similar: "Yea, behold, I will tell you in your mind and in your heart, by the Holy Ghost, which shall come upon you and which shall dwell in your heart.

"Now, behold, this is the spirit of revelation; behold, this is the spirit by which Moses brought the children of Israel through the Red Sea on dry ground." (D&C 8:2-3.)

The Lord can aid in the thinking process while one is considering alternatives. He can cause good feelings inside as the thoughts lead in the right direction. A combination of mind and heart, or thought and feeling, steers the inquirer in the right direction. This may at times be less perceptible than the "burning" witness previously mentioned.

Given experience, the Lord expects the saints to strive to become so finely tuned to communicating with Heavenly Father that the answers may be perceived even when the witness comes in the mildest sense. The Lord's answers tend to be "whispered" rather than "shouted."

What does one do when the counsel of these scriptures is followed but a confirming answer does not come? The first step is to examine one's life and make certain that sin is not blocking the communication channel of the Spirit. These may be sins of omission or commission. If one's life is in order and the answer still does not come, then one must use personal abilities to reach the best-appearing solution and then, with a prayer for guidance, make the decision when it is required by the demands of everyday living. If this has happened in your experience, it may be that the Lord knew you would make the right choice, and wanted you to use your abilities and agency to stand on your own, thus gaining experience and confidence.

4. Health problems pose another source for trials. It is very discouraging to be ill for long periods of time. In dealing with trials of this source

one should ask, "Can I change it?" If the answer is yes, then do so. Proper medical attention, diet, exercise, etc., may be employed to eliminate the trial. If the answer is no, then one must live with the trial without separating from the gospel.

Bishop Baker, a prime example to me in my youth, was stricken with physical problems that left him a cripple in pain throughout his final years of mortality. He, like Job, remained faithful and obedient, and upon entering the doorway of death, I am sure that his physical trials turned to the triumph of immortal victory. When dealing with uncorrectable trials of this nature, the perspective of immortality coupled with humble endurance helps immeasurably.

5. The trial in the death of a loved one may also be so treated. The reasons for the passing may never be known or understood in mortality. Faith, humility, trust in the Lord, and the perspective of immortality can soften the blow until that day comes when all things will be understood.

A close personal friend of mine was killed in what appeared to be a tragic accident. Upon receipt of the news, I entered my office and knelt in prayer. The prayer was broken by sobs, and I ceased to speak until the tears could flow no longer. Then I asked, "Why, Heavenly Father, why?"

I got up from my knees and sat in my chair. Thoughts began to come into my mind that answered why. I quickly got a pen and began writing them down. When I had finished, I knew that my friend had received a call to return home. I wrote that if one could see the vast multitude of spirits that my friend was about to influence, it would bring both awe and amazement.

I gained the assurance that God was at the helm and all would be well. I left things in His hands and tried to honor my friend by living the gospel to the best of my ability and avoiding the bitterness of rebellion. Someday, perhaps, I can gain deeper and clearer insight into the question of why he had to leave when he did. But not now . . . not in mortality.

6. There are trials caused by others (see D&C 124:49-50). The first home my wife and I purchased was burglarized just as we were moving in. Most of our items of value were taken while we were in the moving process. As I reached for the key to the door in the carport, I noticed wood shavings at my feet. "No" I thought, "it can't be!" But it was. As I entered, I found our belongings had been sorted and the items of greater value were missing. What could I do?

I recalled the example of the Savior, who had power to retaliate but did not. I remembered Brother Kempton, who had ordained me a High Priest. He told of how he had come to forgive the men who had murdered his father.

I knelt upon the kitchen floor before calling the police. I said, "Heavenly Father, I forgive whoever did this. Thou mayest deal with them as Thou seest fit."

I never found out what happened to our belongings or the thieves. I did find out that we could recover much easier without the canker of bitterness.

There are unavoidable mental and emotional wounds caused by others, such as the unfaithful husband who deserts his wife and children who are faithful in the church. In such a trial, the first priority is similar to first aid: one figuratively "stops the bleeding, maintains the breathing, and preserves life" until healing evolves with time and careful nourishment. Though the pain is great, it must be endured as best as possible until self-worth is restored and the bitterness of hatred removed.

A desire for revenge or punishment to the offender is not a good first aid treatment. The Lord will deal with the offenders in His own way and time. It is for the offended to forgive and forget, holding onto the iron rod of the gospel. Those who offend and are not dealt with appropriately in this life will surely sow as they reap, and such will be detected and cut off in the next life (D&C 50:7-8).

7. The occurrences of daily living bring trials such as accidents, sunburn, failure due to poor choices, lack of preparation, etc. For those trials that stem from mistakes—don't repeat them!

A shortcut to overcoming trials from this source is to learn from the mistakes of others. This is one of the great values of the scriptures. One can read about the path others have chosen and evaluate the end results; then a value decision can be made that leads to the pursuing of the path that best leads to happiness.

8. I like to toss in one more category in the source of trials: bad luck. That seems to sneak in occasionally to lend a blow in the battle of life. In such perfunctory blows, react as though you weren't selected again in the Reader's Digest drawing. Life goes on.

When one does not recognize the source of a trial, a prayerful self-analysis might be in order as a safety check to determine if the trial is self-caused. A simple flow chart for study might run as follows:

Is there a known cause? "Yes." Is it correctable? "Yes." Then do it!

Many a trial could be removed by that simple process.

If the cause is not known, but could stem from the individual, questions like these could be in order:

Am I 100% committed to the gospel? Do I study the scriptures daily? Do I have regular daily and family prayers? Is my church attendance 100% when I'm well? Are my donations and offerings to the Lord sufficient? Are we holding family home evenings? Am I doing my best to keep harmony and love in the family? Can I feel the Spirit of the Lord?

Such a series of questions often uncovers the source of a correctable trial. If not, prayer and meditation may produce an understanding needed in dealing with the difficulty.

If, through analysis, the answers to the questions on faithfulness are all "yes," then keep on doing your best and be patient. Perhaps patience itself is the quality needing strength.

Though no one will likely perceive with clarity the sources and solutions to all trials (for this would destroy the effect of faith in our mortal test), yet a partial understanding can provide a tempered weapon in the struggle for perfection. The example of others can lend strength and quick action directed toward turning trials into triumphs.

The Lord has promised, ". . . Blessed is he that keepeth my commandments, whether in life or in death; and he that is faithful in tribulation, the reward of the same is greater in the kingdom of heaven.

"Ye cannot behold with your natural eyes, for the present time, the design of your God concerning those things which shall come hereafter, and the glory which shall follow after much tribulation.

"For after much tribulation come the blessings." (D&C 58:2-4.)

CHAPTER FIVE

Going The Second Gospel Mile: Running Or Jogging?

"And whosoever shall compel thee to go a mile, go with him twain." (Matthew 5:41.) Perhaps the concept of going the second mile came from this scripture. The context is a little disconcerting, however, because it appears to be the result of force and follows a verse talking about a legal suit. Since it is the free will offering that counts most (not the forced gift of service), perhaps there is another way of looking at this "second-mile scripture" that fits within the context of a freely given gift of service.

What might "compelling to go the first mile" represent? Perhaps it symbolically represents the minimum standard expected as duty within an office or assignment. There are, attendant to every calling, certain suggested standards to work toward, specified meetings to hold and attend, individuals to work with, etc. Those expected experiences could constitute the "compelled" element of a calling, the first mile; not that the individual is forced to do something against free will, but that one would anticipate or expect that the individual would accomplish "at least" that much within the calling.

Going the second mile, then, could be viewed as doing something beyond the minimum expected performance. It could represent the ingenuity of the member in doing a little extra, such as making the required meeting exceptionally interesting and spiritual, accomplishing the required task with an extra measure of enthusiasm and concern, or adding a complementary addition to the basic framework of the assignment. One meets the minimum standards of achievement (the compelled portion), and then does a little extra to enhance the stewardship (the second-mile portion). The second mile is initiated by the individual, not the presiding officer, and is carried out in the spirit of love, not compulsion.

It is of value to ask why one should be concerned about going the second mile, both in gospel service and personal gospel growth. The answer to such a question would indicate that the second mile is more than a little "nicety;" it is of critical concern to Latter-day Saints.

Why should we be concerned about going the second mile? Because it will have a direct effect upon our happiness in the next life. Our post-mortal status will be determined by our performance as measured by the "second mile."

A sample illustration is provided in the Doctrine and Covenants in the area of having a testimony. Of the Terrestrial beings it is recorded: "These are they who are not valiant in the testimony of Jesus; wherefore, they obtain not the crown over the kingdom of our God." (D&C 76:79.)

These individuals attained the first mile in the acquisition of a testimony, but failed the second mile because they were not valiant with it. Those in the Celestial kingdom also attained testimonies (the first mile), but they went on to achieve the second mile labeled as "valiancy" in testimonies. This is an indication of the differentiation factor between terrestrial and celestial beings who have complied with the basic gospel principles and ordinances. Celestial beings kept going beyond the "first-mile" concept to the second; terrestrial beings did not.

How do these kingdom gradations fit in with happiness? Because the higher the kingdom attained, the greater the happiness acquired.

If one were to take a survey on the street and ask bypassers questions concerning celestial merit, exaltation, or eternal lives, the responses would probably vary from questioning frowns to answers indicating that the average person has little information or opinion concerning the subject. But suppose one were to ask those passers by, "If you could choose your state in a life after death, would you choose to be happy or unhappy?" Assuming they took the question seriously, there is little doubt that normal individuals would choose "happy."

To question further: "Just how happy would you like to be? Extremely happy? moderately happy? or just a little bit happy?"

Most individuals would "shoot for the top." "How happy can I be? I'll take the happiest possible condition."

The happiest possible condition is to be attained in the highest degree of the celestial kingdom. When we talk about celestial life, exaltation, or eternal life, we are really talking about happiness. A good, simple connotative definition for exaltation is: Exaltation = Happiness. Want to be more specific? Then: Exaltation = Your Happiness.

That's what we're qualifying for when we go the second mile, or strive for valiancy.

In working toward that goal of happiness and exaltation, faithful Latter-day Saints are striving for perfection. The ultimate goal was expressed in the command "Therefore I would that ye should be perfect even as I, or your Father who is in heaven is perfect." (3 Nephi 12:48.) Perfection is at the end of the road for "second milers."

Is perfection really an attainable goal?

The answer is yes.

How do we know?

A simple answer is, "Because it is a commandment." Nephi explained, "I will go and do the things which the Lord hath commanded, *for I know that the Lord giveth no commandments unto the children of men, save he shall prepare a way for them that they may accomplish the thing which he commandeth them.*" (1 Nephi 3:7, italics added.)

How, then, should we view our current inadequacies that block perfection?

We should view them as necessary and appropriate constituents of mortal experience, which inadequacies can be overcome. Because there is ". . . an opposition in all things . . ." (2 Nephi 2:11), weakness enters the picture (the opposite of strength). The Lord understood this and explained, "If men come unto me I will show unto them their weakness. I give unto men weakness that they may be humble; and my grace is sufficient for all men that humble themselves before me; for if they humble themselves before me, and have faith in me, then will I make weak things become strong unto them." (Ether 12:27.)

Often we do not need special help in finding our weaknesses. They are all too apparent. Other times, we do need help.

Before leaving on my mission, I was to be set apart by a general authority. My family and I (along with two or three other missionaries and their families) were gathered together in a room in the Church Office Building. I was the first to be set apart. The general authority placed his hands upon my head, set me apart, and began a special blessing. In the middle of the blessing he paused, then said, "And Elder Farley, I say unto you, cease to profane." After another pause, he continued the blessing. I did not open my eyes to look around; had I done so I am sure there would have been some mouths hanging open in shock.

I think I only said one bad word in my life prior to that blessing, and that was before age eight, so perhaps I was safe. Mother thought the general authority had made a mistake. If he had, I thought to myself, maybe he also made a mistake in the blessings he had pronounced upon me. I approached the Lord in prayer and asked why that statement had been made. Because of coming to the Lord, he showed me my weakness. It was not long before I realized that although I didn't say profane words, they would often flash into my mind. (It may have been the aftermath of conditioning in military basic training which I had just completed prior to my setting apart.) When I realized what my weakness was, I began working on it. With the help and grace of the Lord, intermingled with time and occasional frustration, I was able to overcome the problem and become strong in that area, as the scripture had promised.

As we overcome weaknesses, we progress toward the goal of perfection and the attainment of greater personal happiness. (This happiness is both a mortal achievement and an eternal reward.) The "second mile" is a key factor in our growth patterns.

Perfection, then, is possible. Of course, the fullest attainment cannot come until post-mortality, but it is possible to reach a state called perfection within mortal limitations. Of Noah it is recorded, "And thus Noah found grace in the eyes of the Lord; for Noah was a just man, and perfect in his generation. . . ." (Moses 8:27.)

President Kimball explained that ". . . Progress toward eternal life is a matter of achieving perfection . . . Being perfect means to triumph over sin. This is a mandate from the Lord. He is just and wise and kind. He would never require anything from his children which was not for their benefit and which was not attainable. Perfection therefore is an achievable goal."*

Knowing of the possibility of attainment and having the example of someone from scriptural accounts who did achieve, it is easier to become motivated to seek the second mile of service and accomplishment in order to reach our goals and keep the commandment to become perfect.

Ever wonder how long will it take to achieve the type of perfection necessary to become like our Heavenly Father? No one knows, and the time would certainly vary for different individuals, but we are not left without an example in this area.

Speaking of Abraham, Isaac and Jacob, the Lord revealed that ". . . because they did none other things than that which they were commanded, they have entered into their exaltation, according to the promises, and sit upon thrones, and are not angels but are gods." (D&C 132:37.)

These three individuals achieved that state in the period of time between their mortal lives and the date of this revelation. That gives at least a general perspective of hope to which we may look. The scripture indicates that they achieved that status by doing ". . . none other things than that which they were commanded. . . ." (D&C 132:37.) This would indicate that they did not vary from the path of the gospel into the devious paths of the world, but applied gospel principles in overcoming weaknesses and progressing toward the goal they now have attained. We may assume that they became valiant, that they strove for the second mile by using free agency to

---

*Spencer W. Kimball, *The Miracle of Forgiveness* (Salt Lake City, Utah: Bookcraft Publishers, 1969), pp. 208-209.

choose appropriate actions leading toward perfection. The Lord did not tell them everything to do.

"For behold, it is not meet that I should command in all things; for he that is compelled in all things, the same is a slothful and not a wise servant; wherefore he receiveth no reward.

"Verily I say, men should be anxiously engaged in a good cause, and do many things of their own free will, and bring to pass much righteousness;

"For the power is in them, wherein they are agents unto themselves." (D&C 58:26-28.)

Within that scripture is the motivation and justification for the second mile. The first mile (and less) in achievement is alluded to in the next verse: "But he that doeth not anything until he is commanded, and receiveth a commandment with doubtful heart, and keepeth it with slothfulness, the same is damned." (D&C 58:29.) The first mile must lead to the second.

With a concept of the importance and final results of going the second mile, what does one do to qualify?

The first step is the psychological commitment. Knowing it is possible to reach a goal is very important. Let's theoretically take a young man who is just learning to play basketball, and give him the challenge to make twenty baskets in a row from the free throw line. Let's assume that he believes that it really is possible for him to make twenty baskets in a row, and he begins to practice. Let's also assume that we keep a record of his progress over a period of time until he attains the goal.

Let's assume, now that we have our theoretical practice record on file, that we move time backwards and approach the same boy in the same way, with the only difference being that he really doesn't believe it is possible to make twenty baskets in a row. However, he does put in the same amount of practice time. If we could compare his practice record of achievement in this case with the record theoretically kept in the first example (where he believed the goal was attainable), it is almost certain that we would note a significant difference in the achievement of the young man. The practice record kept when he believed in the goal would likely be impressively better than when he disbelieved. (This principle probably indicates why Nephi got the brass plates of Laban instead of Laman or Lemuel.)

Positive mental attitude, and belief in achievement of a goal (or commandment), puts one within the realm of the second mile.

I recall the first table tennis game I played with my father. I had developed an interest in the game, so he obtained a table and equipment and we began to play. The final score of the first game was something like 21-0 in his favor. We played a second game with the same results. In fact, over the next several games his final score remained a constant 21 while mine varied from 0 to 3 points. I believed, however, that I could win a game and was psychologically committed to attain that goal.

The weeks passed by and my score began to climb. First I reached 4 or 5 points, then 10 or 12, and eventually 15 or 16. Finally the day came when I won. It was a good, honest win, with no handicaps given to me by my father.

From that point on I seldom lost, and the long climb led to two table tennis championships in junior and senior high schools. If I had not believed it was ever possible to reach a state where I could win a game with my father, it is unlikely that my record would have come anywhere near what it did.

In a gospel setting, what will the record of progress be for one who really believes it is possible to become perfect and is psychologically committed, as compared with one of similar potential who really doesn't believe it is possible to become perfect, especially not in this life? Think of the edge that will be lost by the one who lacks the belief and psychological commitment for the higher ideal.

Thus, mental commitment to an ideal and a belief in the possibility of attainment are important factors in achieving that important "second mile." This is true in the attainment of spiritual goals, and magnification of a calling, just as it is true in the attainment of temporal goals.

When one has the faith to make such a commitment, one must then follow through with the actions. "But wilt thou know, O vain man, that faith without works is dead?" (James 2:20.) Nephi said, ". . . I will go and do . . ." (1 Nephi 3:7.) He did not say "*tomorrow* I will go and do," or "*sometime* I will go and do," or "*later* I will go and do." Neither was he concerned about the amount of time it would take to achieve what he was going to do. He did not say "I will go and do for one week," or month, or year; he said "I will go and do," and he went and did. That's the commitment second milers need.

Now comes the important question concerning running or jogging. "How fast should I be *going* and *doing*?"

An example might help in answering this question.

As a college student, I took some classes in physical training, including boxing and karate. I enjoyed the exercise very much. I was able to workout with vigor and intensity over a given length of time. After college graduation and marriage, I let the workouts go and, of course, lost the edge of physical agility and strength I previously had.

About ten years later, I decided to resurrect myself physically and so enrolled in a karate class. I sought quickly the same intensity and vigor I had in my college days, and thought that I had attained it. My peak was short lived, however. During a workout period, I injured my right shoulder because it was not ready for the amount of strain I was placing upon it. It had handled that amount of strain very well in college days, but it was not in condition any more for that level of usage. The result was that I lost over a year's time of full use of the entire arm because of the pain of a pulled ligament. It cost me the workout periods, the sport, and the normal use of my arm. I had to drop back to an elementary level of exercise after a sufficient period of rest for the injured shoulder. I had tried to do too much too soon. The end result was not rapid advancement, but a loss of time and ability.

Service within the church and attainment of personal goals in the pathway of gospel progress could end up with the same disappointing results if one tries to do too much too soon. Take the convert who joins the church and says "I'm going to be just like the missionaries—by next month" and is soon inactive in the church. What about the church officer who spends so much time counseling members that he fails with his own wife and children? Consider the Relief Society sister who worries so much about great success with her calling that nervousness and perhaps ulcers retire her from service.

The Prophet Joseph Smith explained: "When you climb up a ladder, you must begin at the bottom, and ascend step by step, until you arrive at the top; and so it is with the principles of the gospel—you must begin with the first, and go on until you learn all the principles of exaltation. But it will be a great while after you have passed through the veil before you will have learned them. It is not all to be comprehended in this world; it will be a great work to learn our salvation and exaltation even beyond the grave."*

Walking must precede running; in infant stages, crawling must precede even walking. The principle of progress is the same within the gospel. A convert just coming into the church would not participate with the intensity and speed that a trained and experienced member would; yet the convert could be a second miler in his own right.

It is not necessary to compete with the best in order to go beyond the minimum requirements of one's current level of progress. If the convert's gospel life were compared to someone who recently decided to begin a program of running, a sequence might develop like this. First comes a physical examination to determine capabilities and detect danger areas. If there are no problem areas, or if problem areas are detected and corrected, the exercise program might begin with walking short distances at moderate paces. When the body is appropriately conditioned and trained at these early levels, the increase of pace and progress to jogging might occur. Eventually, distance and pace would increase until one is comfortable running without injuring the body. This is an important element in reaching physical goals: when one has properly progressed to a specified level, achievement at that level will not produce injuries or unnecessary strain on the body.

---

*Joseph Smith, *History of the Church* (Salt Lake City, Utah: Deseret Book Company, 1978), Vol. 6, pp. 306-307.

Spiritual development is much the same. One must have a "spiritual" examination to determine current levels of capability as well as problem areas. Instead of trying to immediately match the service levels of the bishop or stake president, the convert would progress a step at a time to correct problem areas and begin a program of development conducive to his current condition. Prayers, scripture study, family harmony, payment of tithes and offerings, church attendance, holding of family home evening, etc., would be areas included in the spiritual training program (though there are minimum levels of achievement necessary to be worthy for church membership). If the convert shows valiancy in his efforts (going beyond current levels of achievement as motivated by love, yet avoiding injury from overstraining) he is a second miler, even though there are others around who are doing more. Eventually he may attain the levels of service reached by other valiant members, but it will be a result of proper step-by-step development, and not a sudden "burst of speed to the top." The scriptural counsel is: "And see that all these things are done in wisdom and order; for it is not requisite that a man should run faster than he has strength." (Mosiah 4:27.)

This does not mean that one can leave out certain areas within the principles and ordinances of the gospel. Everyone is capable of living the minimum standards required for church membership. If a weakness exists as a hinderance, the Lord will provide the necessary help to overcome the obstacle if approached by the worthy member or investigator. Each member should live within the realm of acceptable sainthood (the first mile), but the levels and rates of additional progress (the second mile) will vary with the individuals and their conditions. Each Latter-day Saint, having made the commitment for improvement, will begin by going a little beyond current capacity (without straining and causing injury), then getting conditioned at that level, and then moving ahead. The process is repeated until each individual reaches his own prime (not someone else's). Progress should be measured against previous personal attainments, without comparisons to one's neighbor's progress.

When an individual does reach a prime condition in any one area (church service, scripture study, keeping personal journals, etc.), he will feel good. He will have become conditioned and, like an athlete, will enjoy his work without undue stress and strain. Though he may often feel tired at the end of a period of service, yet he will feel capable and generally exhilarated, not exhausted and beaten. In addition, his success in one area will not come at the expense of another necessary area in his own life, or in the lives of his loved ones. For example, a father who spends hours studying the scriptures on Monday evening and does not get around to holding family home evening has not reached a prime in either area.

When a saint reaches a level of development where there are no apparent weaknesses needing correction (an attainable state), the challenge then becomes one of endurance. As Nephi explained, "And now, my beloved brethren, after ye have gotten into this straight and narrow path, I would ask if all is done? Behold, I say unto you, Nay, for ye have not come thus far save it were by the word of Christ with unshaken faith in him, relying wholly upon the merits of him who is mighty to save.

"Wherefore, ye must press forward with a steadfastness in Christ, having a perfect brightness of hope, and a love of God and of all men. Wherefore, if ye shall press forward, feasting upon the word of Christ, and endure to the end, behold, thus saith the Father: Ye shall have eternal life." (2 Nephi 31:19-20.)

For those saints who do endure and press forward, the positive attributes of sainthood are deepened and intensified, and abilities to serve are developed to greater degrees with experience.

There are four major areas that need concurrent development throughout the stages of attainment within the first and second miles. Though there is a hierarchy of priority, no area may be left out or sacrificed for the development of the others. These areas are (1) self, (2) family, (3) church, and (4) profession.

Putting "self" at the head of the list does not mean that one is to become self-centered. It means that unless an individual can keep himself on the proper spiritual track, he will not likely be able to influence his wife and family properly. The mother must be personally stable in order to be of influence to her husband and children. One's own spirituality must be growing before others can be motivated by the example.

When "self" is in the proper perspective, influence upon the family is a natural outgrowth of gospel commitment. The home is the basic unit within the kingdom of God. No service anywhere in the world is more important than the service within the home. Family prayers, home evenings, love and unity, etc., help build an atmosphere conducive to gospel growth.

Next in priority comes the church, the organization designed for the perfection and exaltation of self and family. Total commitment to the church and its programs is necessary for success in the first two areas of priority.

Finally comes the profession. The father (in some instances, the mother) must provide a living by rendering service within the community. Self-support is dignified, and the service within a profession or trade provides growth and stability necessary for a prospering community.

Again, a compatible pace of achievement in all of these areas is a safeguard that one important element will not be lost while striving for another.

In summary, going the second mile represents doing something beyond the expected or required. It is a key factor in the attainment of happiness, both in mortality and post-mortality. It involves commitment, belief in the attainability of a goal, and the actions necessary to accomplish the goal. The actions will occur in proper sequence and degrees of strength compatible with individual talents and abilities. When one is serving properly in the second mile, it will not be a strenuous activity causing injury; it will be a manifestation of conditioning and ability within one's own prime. Second-mile service is measured by self-progress, not competition with others. The individual, the family, the home, and the profession are priority areas of development, and endurance is the quality necessary to bring sainthood to fruition.

CHAPTER SIX

Husbands And Wives In The Gospel

Picture a set of young children you love. The picture may be of your own children, grandchildren, a friend's children, or any other group of children that draws the feelings of your heart.

Now imagine this. You have just been told that the marriage of their parents is ending with a divorce. The announcement is sudden. You did not know it was coming. Neither do the children. As a home or visiting teacher, you have been approached with the assignment to call the children together and inform them of the divorce. The father has already left the premises and the mother is too filled with emotion to be able to tell the children without losing control.

You meet the mother and small children in their living room. The mother announces that you have something important to explain to the children. She sits quietly, head bowed. The children all look attentively at you. How will you tell them? What will be your first words? Imagine the look in the eyes of the children as you inform them that their daddy doesn't love their mommy anymore, and has decided not to be the father in the home. How would you feel inside as you continued on? How do you think the children would react?

If that imagined scene touches your heart, you may appreciate how I felt. The scene was more than an imagined one for me. I told the children, watched the looks in their eyes as the tears welled up, and sat in frustration when they asked why. I saw them gather around the mother, together, yet alone, bewildered and stung with the news of the separation. I returned home with a new commitment to my marriage and family, having lived vicariously a portion of the anguish they faced in reality.

What does it take to produce a marriage? Only a husband and a wife.

What does it take to produce a good Latter-day Saint marriage? A faithful husband and wife sealed according to priesthood laws. The law and the standard is expressed in the Doctrine and Covenants:

"And again, verily I say unto you, if a man marry a wife by my word, which is my law, and by the new and everlasting covenant, and it is sealed unto them by the Holy Spirit of Promise, by him who is anointed, unto whom I have appointed this power and the keys of this priesthood . . . it shall be done unto them in all things whatsoever my servant hath put upon them, in time, and through all eternity; and shall be of full force when they are out of the world. . . ." (D&C 132:19.)

That is the goal for every Latter-day Saint husband and wife. To be sealed in the temple is vital; even more vital is the necessity of remaining worthy. Just to have the "paper work" done is not enough. The scripture quoted indicated the seal of the Holy Spirit of Promise. Joseph Fielding Smith said:

"*The Holy Spirit of Promise is the Holy Ghost* who places the stamp of approval upon every ordinance: baptism, confirmation, ordination, marriage. *The promise is that the blessings will be received through faithfulness.*

"If a person violates a covenant, whether it be of baptism, ordination, marriage or anything else, the Spirit withdraws the stamp of approval, and the blessings will not be received.

"Every ordinance is sealed with a promise of a reward based upon faithfulness. The Holy Spirit withdraws the stamp of approval where covenants are broken."*

Those whose faithfulness have slipped need quick and committed repentance in order to restore the validity of the sealing ordinance. Those who have remained faithful need to temper security with caution. Two examples will illustrate what I mean.

One of the greats in the hall of faithful saints was the Old Testament David. As a youth, David's faithfulness and strength was exhibited as he killed a lion and a bear to protect his father's sheep. (1 Samuel 17:34-37.) Knowing that the Lord delivered him from these dangers, he knew the Lord could deliver him from the giant enemy, Goliath. Without fear, David answered the giant's rude challenge:

"Thou comest to me with a sword, and with a spear, and with a shield: but I come to thee in the name of the Lord of hosts, the God of the armies of Israel, whom thou has defied." (1 Samuel 17:45.)

---

*Joseph Fielding Smith, *Doctrines Of Salvation* (Compiled by Bruce R. McConkie, Salt Lake City, Utah: Bookcraft Publishers, 1954), Vol. 1, p. 45.

The battle was short: Goliath fell dead at little David's feet. David was committed to the gospel and close to the Lord.

A New Testament figure of comparable faithfulness is Peter. His commitment is noted in the nearing events of Gethsemane, a time of trial far greater than the threat of Goliath.

"And when they had sung an hymn, they went out into the mount of Olives. Then saith Jesus unto them, All ye shall be offended because of me this night: for it is written, I will smite the shepherd, and the sheep of the flock shall be scattered abroad.

"Peter answered and said unto him, Though all men shall be offended because of thee, yet will I never be offended.

". . . Though I should die with thee, yet will I not deny thee." (Matthew 26:31, 33, 35.)

Peter was also committed to the gospel, and close to the Lord.

What were the outcomes of their lives? David fell and lost all that he had (see D&C 132:38-39). Peter, though denying three times, was able to carry on and maintain his station, holding the keys of the kingdom (Matthew 16:15-19) and never losing them, as evidenced by his role in the restoration (see D&C 27:12-13).

What is the lesson as applied to marriage? Two people were committed and faithful; only one finished the course. Two marriages may start out right; only one may finish the course.

Current success within a marriage is a good sign, but not a guarantee of successful completion. The family I described, that broke up, began with a temple marriage.

Not all temple sealings will be valid; only those who continue faithful throughout their lives will be granted the promised blessings. Paul said:

"Brethren, I count not myself to have apprehended: but this one thing I do, forgetting those things which are behind, and reaching forth unto those things which are before.

"I press toward the mark for the prize of the high calling of God in Christ Jesus.

"Let us therefore, as many as be perfect, be thus minded: . . ." (Philippians 3:13-15.)

Those most committed to successful marriages will be actively building the marriage relationship, and will not maintain a false sense of security or an unfounded assumption that "all is well."

A wonderful example of willingness for evaluation and change is given in the scriptures. It occurred on the eve of the atonement.

"And in the evening he cometh with the twelve.

"And as they sat and did eat, Jesus said, Verily I say unto you, One of you which eateth with me shall betray me.

"And they began to be sorrowful, and to say unto him one by one, Is it I? and another said, Is it I?" (Mark 14:17-19.)

The apostles, most committed to the gospel and closest of all men to the Lord, when informed that someone would be untrue, asked, "Is it I?" They did not respond, "Certainly it would not be one of us." They looked in introspection, and queried in evaluation, "Is it I?" Their position was not an assumption of guaranteed success, but of hope toward faithfulness.

In a similar way, a temple recommend does not assure one of eternal life and marriage; neither does the ordinance of sealing alone. Current success must be monitered with the same attitude of the apostles: Are we faithful? Can we do more?

With the attitude of continuing success born of the hope for eternal union, consistency of gospel living is a vital element. The advice given by Nephi can well be applied to one's marital success:

"And now, my beloved brethren, after ye have gotten into this straight and narrow path, I would ask if all is done? Behold, I say unto you, Nay; for ye have not come thus far save it were by the word of Christ with unshaken faith in him, relying wholly upon the merits of him who is mighty to save.

"Wherefore, ye must press forward with a steadfastness in Christ, having a perfect brightness of hope, and a love of God and of all men. Wherefore, if ye shall press forward, feasting upon the word of Christ, and endure to the end, behold, thus saith the Father: Ye shall have eternal life." (2 Nephi 31:19-20.)

Those with successful marriages must continue to build and endure. Of all the institutions of society, marriage deserves the most care and development. This suggests that church members, while being positive, should not adopt an attitude that says, "We've got it made, all we have to do is coast." Couples should emphasize the need for introspection and continuing effort to keep a happy marriage going.

Satan, through rebellion, lost the privileges of both mortality and immortality. Among other things, marriage and family relationships would never be his. Having lost mortal opportunities, he became miserable, and now seeks to pass that misery on to others. "And because he had fallen from heaven, and had become miserable forever, he sought also the misery of all mankind." (2 Nephi 2:18.) One of the targets in his campaign for misery is the marriage relationship. One of his most widely used tools is the one he used against David: temptations of immorality.

One husband I counseled confessed that he had problems controlling his thoughts. His excuse was that he felt he was different than others in that he had stronger physical drives, and thus greater pressures. We read together the following two scriptures:

"Let no man say when he is tempted, I am tempted of God: for God cannot be tempted with evil, neither tempteth he any man:

"But every man is tempted, when he is drawn away of his own lust, and enticed.

"Then when lust hath conceived, it bringeth forth sin: and sin, when it is finished, bringeth forth death.

"Do not err, my beloved brethren." (James 1:13-16.)

And also, "There hath no temptation taken you but such as is common to man: but God is faithful, who will not suffer you to be tempted above that ye are able; but will with the temptation also make a way to escape, that ye may be able to bear it." (1 Corinthians 10:13.)

He left with a knowledge that others faced similar trials, and that there was a way to overcome temptations rather than fall to them.

I pondered early one morning about the case of David. Such a wonderful man, and yet he fell. If such individuals fall, is there any hope for the rest of us? Where did he slip?

As I pondered, I had the following thoughts come to mind. David fell as a result of not controlling his thoughts. He enjoyed looking when he shouldn't have. One thing led to another, and the thoughts progressed to sin, and that to death (as the scriptures indicate.)

There is a false concept among some members of the church that says, speaking of members of the opposite sex, "It's all right to look at the menu as long as you don't order." David proved that philosophy to be false. Once an individual is married, looking at another person's attractiveness is a dangerous act that could open the door to deadly sin. When you're married, stop looking. It's that simple.

I once asked the girls in a seminary class to do a little experiment. I asked them to quietly situate themselves in a hallway of the school during class change and watch the eyes of the high school boys as a girl walked by. When the experiment was over, the girls did not feel complimented with such attention. They also had a key to look for in seeking the right kind of a young man to associate with.

The battle against sin is fought and won within the mind. Some of the best men have fallen when the mind became an incubator for questionable thoughts.

I asked the boys of the class to watch themselves when they looked at the girls. I told them that the key to safety (which applies equally well to older men) is to look eye level or above. That may seem funny at first, but it works. I suggested that if any boy had difficulty keeping his eyes in the right place, he was to kick himself in the shins. If that didn't work, kick harder the next time. A couple of students really appreciated that adivce, for it set them on a new track of thought control, though it took awhile for their shins to heal.

Movies, television shows, and magazines peddle temptations in bulk. It is easiest to resist them before they are taken in. Simply don't buy or allow questionable books or shows to infiltrate the family.

Sometimes Satan subtly works on the husband or wife with the suggested question, "I wonder if I'm still attractive enough to catch someone else's attention?" If pursued, that thought could explode, causing damages and injury not anticipated. Attractiveness is an asset meant for the spouse, unintended for peddling before other members of the opposite sex.

The change of one's figure as life progresses sometimes poses a problem for the spouse. I knew a man who divorced his wife because she gained sufficient weight to destroy her pre-marriage figure. No rationalization on earth or in eternity will justify that man in his actions.

Satan has become so open in peddling lustful practices that he has infiltrated the marriage relationship itself. Some feel that once you're married, anything physical you want to do with each other is acceptable. That philosophy is wrong—dead wrong. The Latter-day Saint couple cannot imitate the world in physical practices. There are limits beyond which the married couple cannot go and maintain the Spirit of the Lord.

The kingdoms of glory in the next phase of our existence are differentiated by the symbols of the sun, the moon, and the stars. Individuals in this life might well be characterized by their faithfulness within the same categories. Celestial-type people will be more faithful than terrestrial or telestial people. The level followed on earth will be the level received in fulness as the reward after mortality.

"They who are of a celestial spirit shall receive the same body which was a natural body; even ye shall receive your bodies, and your glory shall be that glory by which your bodies are quickened.

"Ye who are quickened by a portion of the celestial glory shall then receive of the same, even a fulness.

"And they who are quickened by a portion of the terrestrial glory shall then receive of the same, even a fulness.

"And they who remain shall also be quickened; nevertheless, they shall return again to their own place, to enjoy that which they are willing to receive, because they were not willing to enjoy that which they might have received." (D&C 88:28-32.)

How would the prayers of a celestial-type person differ from a terrestrial type? The celestial person would likely pray longer, more frequently, and with deeper feeling and intent to listen for answers than the telestial person who might pray sporadically, if at all.

The celestial person would excel in standards above those other groups who, by their own choices, become more lax in righteousness. It is the same in marital physical relationships. The celestially motivated marriage couple will not participate in all of the sexual acts indulged in by the world. There will be a higher standard.

The physical relationship in marriage (properly used) must be viewed as good, designed by a wise Heavenly Father. Such closeness bonds husband and wife and maintains love and loyalty. When acts foreign to normal physical relationships begin to replace love with feelings of lust, giving the body authority over the mind, a celestial relationship is lost. Couples in marriage should prayerfully seek to enjoy each other within the boundaries set by the inspiration of the Lord.

There will be other Satanical challenges hurled at the marriage relationship. There will also be threats from non-Satanical forces when unexpected problems occur in the marriage. Too often many spouses rush to the "specialist" when difficulties arise. They look for impressive titles on office doors, and fancy labels for abstract psychological problems that relieve them of the burden of responsibility. Most problems ought to be solved individually by the husband and wife. The greatest role of a counselor is to convince husbands and wives that they have the ability themselves to change their lives and correct their own problems. Husbands and wives must assume the responsibility for the success of their own marriages and not drop their problems at the feet of a counselor unless such professional help is really appropriate, which will be the minority of the time.

When a Latter-day Saint couple is having difficulties and divorce becomes a threat, it is a good sign that the gospel standards have not been consistently maintained in the lives of the husband and wife.

President Harold B. Lee stated: ". . .Likewise, if in that Latter-day Saint home the husband and wife are in disharmony, bickering, and divorce is threatened, there is an evidence that one or both are not keeping the commandments of God."*

Joseph Fielding Smith said that "If a man and his wife were earnestly and faithfully observing all the ordinances and principles of the gospel, there could not arise any cause for divorce. . . ."†

What can a couple do to help insure a successful marriage and avoid the pitfalls of degeneracy? Paul counseled "Nevertheless neither is the man without the woman, neither the woman without the man, in the Lord." (1 Corinthians 11:11.) The Lord's program calls for marriage; the marriage program calls for the Lord. There is a trinity in the marriage covenant. Paul stated it this way:

"Wives, submit yourselves unto your own husbands, as unto the Lord."

"For the husband is the head of the wife, even as Christ is the head of the church: and he is the savior of the body."

*Conference Report, April 1950, pp. 97-98.
†Improvement Era, June 1965, p. 495.

"Therefore as the church is subject unto Christ, so let the wives be to their own husbands in every thing."

"Husbands, love your wives, even as Christ also loved the church, and gave himself for it." (Ephesians 5:22-25.)

The ideal model is a marriage relationship where the wife can totally trust her husband, knowing he will love her more than his own life. In submitting herself to him, she knows that every act of the husband will be for her benefit, protection, growth and security. The husband will love his wife as the Savior loves the church; she will be his most prized stewardship, and he will love, comfort, and direct according to principles of righteousness. When the wife follows the husband, she knows she is following the Lord, for the husband is striving to do what the Lord would have him do. It is a glorious concept. It is the perfect model for marriage. In following such a guide, a oneness of love and purpose will weld the husband and wife together into an eternal unit, to be glorified by the Lord whom they took as their guide.

As the marriage matures in years and experiences, we must work and sacrifice to maintain the warmth and respect that flourished during courtship. The excitement of just being together, the opportunity to go special places as a couple, little courtesies of love such as the note in the lunchbox, the flower handed to the wife, etc., can be preserved and continued.

Some of the warmest expressions of love between a husband and wife come in a letter when the two are apart. The letters thus created become keepsakes, momentos of love to be cherished forever.

Couples don't have to be apart to share such letters. Instead of waiting for the business trip or other activity to provide the setting for such letters, the husband and wife can select a day to write each other a love letter. They will each write while alone, as if apart for a few days. The husband may write during a break at work, the wife sometime during a break in her day. Only warm, positive feelings are written; nothing negative is allowed into the picture. At the close of the day, each spouse gives the love letter to the other. They read what each other wrote, then share feelings and expressions of appreciation verbally.

In doing this, the marriage partners will sense a renewed glow from courtship days and a greater enjoyment of their love.

If the husband, particularly, can get past the first hurdle of saying "that's silly," or "my wife already knows how I feel," a rich experience lies in store for the marriage. If both partners center on the positive aspects of their marriage and begin expressing them in love-letter-style, the results will be very rewarding. Doors for expression of feelings and positive communication will open up.

Another way to renew the warmth and respect of courtship days is to follow the counsel repeated by the scriptures to "remember your heritage."

The children of Israel were often reminded to recall how the Lord had led them out of Egypt and had preserved them. In the Book of Mormon we are counseled to ". . . remember how merciful the Lord hath been unto the children of men, from the creation of Adam even down unto the time that ye shall receive these things, . . ." (Moroni 10:3.) Our general conferences will repeat the Joseph Smith story and the message of the restoration. Our national holidays proclaim a fourth of July, etc. On the twenty-fourth of July we remember our pioneer heritage.

How is all of this applied to the marriage relationship? Sometime when the husband and wife have some quiet moments together, they should remember their heritage that brought them together. Each may take time to verbally review how he or she felt when meeting and falling in love with the other. Recall the time when each was certain that the right one had been found, how they became engaged, what it was like the day of the marriage. In reviewing and sharing these beautiful moments, the warmth of early courtship days seems to renew and take on an even brighter glow. It provides a rich rejuvenation for the husband and wife, and little courtesies of love and respect often begin to "pop up" in areas where they had been forgotten (like opening doors for the wife, holding hands, saying "thank you," etc.).

I know personally that family units can continue in eternity for those who are worthy. Some years ago I was standing with my wife in the celestial room of the Salt Lake Temple. A temple matron approached us and asked if we would stand in vicariously for a family sealing. We indicated that we would be happy to and were then ushered into one of the sealing rooms of the temple. The sealer introduced himself to us and spent a few moments explaining the nature of the sealing ordinance. He indicated that he had been taught by the temple president that in more cases than one might expect, the spirits of those for whom the sealing ordinances are being performed are present to witness the event. He asked us to keep that in mind as we participated in the sealing of the family for which they had the records.

I knelt on one side of the altar representing the husband. An elderly woman knelt on the other side representing the wife. My wife represented the daughter, and a gentleman whom I did not know represented the son.

The ceremony was performed in behalf of the parents. Then came the time for my wife to kneel in behalf of the first child. When the name of that child was read prefacing the sealing prayer, I unmistakably felt the presence of that individual as she came forward, unseen by mortal eyes. My impressions were so strong that she had come forward and was standing near the altar that I greeted her mentally by repeating her name in my mind. When I did so, the impression came back to me that she was aware that I knew she was there, and she returned an acknowledgment and a thank you. When the prayer was concluded, her presence left. The next child's name was read, and again I felt that person step forward to the altar for the service. I again repeated the name of the individual and again felt the presence and acknowledgment of thanks. This occurred with every child in the family until the work of sealing was concluded. I never opened my eyes to look up; yet I knew by the feelings of the Spirit that they were present in the sealing room of the temple.

The family can be an eternal unit; it should be. Every husband and wife can qualify to be together forever, eternally happy, sealed by the priesthood which is recognized in both time and eternity. That should be the goal of husbands and wives in the gospel.

CHAPTER SEVEN

Offspring: A Lease With The Option To Buy

There are circumstances in which a person can get into a home without the obligation of purchase, yet inheriting the potential to do so. Hence, an agreement is set up wherein the occupant pays a rental fee for the use of the home as long as he desires to be a renter; if he determines that he wants to become an owner, provisions are made for a conversion from rental to ownership.

This principle is not unlike the concept of parenthood. The beginning parent receives a child on loan from Heavenly Father; the possibility for ownership is inherent in the agreement, but not required. The parent may symbolically "rent" the child for a few years of mortality, then give up the possession and move out of the family circle when the "mortal lease" expires. Where, or when, or if the conversion privilege is opted, depends upon the willingness of the parent to meet the conditions of possession written within the parental contract.

I sensed this beginning impermanency with the birth of our first child, Charlene. Janene and I were living in a small town in Fairfield, Idaho (a population in the mid three hundreds). I had just graduated from college at Brigham Young University and had accepted a contract to teach music in the public schools of this area. We anticipated the birth date to be around the time of the new year, 1969.

We had, as others, studied to become experts. We read and discussed much of what there is to know about something which you've not had the opportunity to participate in knowing about. That's parenthood before it happens.

As the delivery date drew near, so did the winter storms. Snow fell, roads packed over with ice, and the forty-mile drive to the hospital became more and more threatening. A local, retired nurse was summoned to reserve duty, and future mom and dad waited in anxiety for the blessed event to occur.

It came. Not quite like I had anticipated. I've never adjusted well to jumping up in the middle of the night (the time which, I learned through experience, most babies choose to enter mortality—maybe it's the time zone difference between Kolob and earth—they leave in their daylight but arrive in our night). My stomach prefers to get up after dawn. The baby didn't take that into consideration. How long my wife had lain in labor I didn't know, but when the time came (according to what we had read in the books), I got the elbow in the ribs and jumped up in excitement before my stomach was alerted to the sudden change of position. We phoned the doctor in the early hours of the morning and were encouraged to drive to the hospital; not that the pains were that critical as yet, but the roads were. So we left for Haily, Idaho, the town housing the nearest hospital.

Upon arrival, we were informed that we "jumped the gun" a little, but should remain there rather than chance the poor weather and road conditions. So we settled in. Morning passed, lunch time slipped by, and the hours of the afternoon were spent visiting, wondering, and writing the time of each labor pain on the Improvement Era we were reading.

Supper. The doctor told the nurses that if he were needed, he would be at the local high school basketball game in which his son was to play.

By now our fears had been swallowed up in the anxiousness for the delivery to occur. What could we do to hurry the process? My wife had read that a little activity sometimes helped, so we cautiously peered around the corners of the room to see if hospital personnel were present. Finding our corner of the hospital empty, we sneaked out into the hallway and practiced some jitter-bug routines we had learned in college. We had a great time, but when the dance was over, there was no apparent progress toward the delivery.

By now we gave up the anxiety and decided it was a question of endurance. I turned on the only television set in the hospital and became engrossed in a Don Knotts movie. Right when it got to the good part—when everything was getting exciting—it happened. "It's coming," Janene announced!

"Now?" I questioned. "Right in the middle of the movie? Are you sure?"

She was sure, and I gripped the "call button" by the edge of the bed and rang it several times as an expectant father might do. The country nurses came running. Things began to whirl at that point. After coaxing all day, we didn't want it to come right then; the doctor was at a ball game.

I was quickly ushered out, and my request to take the TV was flatly denied. I sat nervously in the waiting room, straining to hear the motor of the doctor's car as it entered the hospital lot. Nervousness turned to anxiety when I heard a nurse saying "Don't let it come yet! Wait for the doctor!" The book I had read said that wasn't the right thing to do. "Oh, hurry up doctor," I plead. "You've got to beat the baby here, or they're going to ruin everything."

A commotion at the end of the hallway told me that the doctor had arrived. Into the delivery room he rushed, then all became still within the range of my ears. The silence was soon broken with the distant cry of a baby; a baby who hadn't been there a few moments before. "It's happened," I thought! "How is my wife?"

A few minutes later I was summoned to the hallway. There was the doctor, wheeling my wife and baby daughter toward her room. I was so concerned about my wife that I virtually missed seeing the baby at her side.

"You can be proud of her," the doctor said of Janene. "She delivered just fine." I was shown a picture of the baby. The doctor had taken the picture by standing on a chair and shooting downward with his polaroid camera (part of the "home-town" service, I supposed).

A brief visit with my wife and she was asleep. I went back to look at the baby I had overlooked before. There she was, cute as ever. But mine? I was still having trouble with the arithmetic. One of my family entered the delivery room and two came out. It was hard to comprehend. But there she was. I was given a feeling, perhaps a message from Heavenly Father. "This child is being loaned to you on a temporary basis. Whether or not you keep her depends entirely upon you. She is my daughter, now given into your care."

I understood clearly. Oh, how I wanted to prove worthy. In my prayers that night I said "Thy" baby daughter, not "mine." I knew that the time could come when I would feel a claim upon her as a child, but it was certain now that I had to prove myself. It was almost like a lease, with the option to buy.

During the next visiting session, I stared at our tiny child. There was a body, made by us, quickened by a spirit daughter of Heavenly Father. I recalled the scripture that said "Remember the worth of souls is great in the sight of God." (D&C 18:10.) Then I thought of the Savior's reaction to the little children on the American hemisphere:

". . . and he took their little children, one by one, and blessed them, and prayed unto the Father for them. And when he had done this he wept again; And he spake unto the multitude, and said unto them: Behold your little ones. And as they looked to behold they cast their eyes towards heaven, and they saw the heavens open, and they saw angels descending out of heaven as it were in the midst of fire; and they came down and encircled those little ones about, and they were encircled about with fire; and the angels did minister unto them." (3 Nephi 17:21-24.)

There was a freshness, a clean atmosphere about the child. I remembered the teaching that ". . . little children are redeemed from the foundation of the world through mine Only Begotten;

"Wherefore, they cannot sin, for power is not given unto Satan to tempt little children, until they begin to become accountable before me." (D&C 30:46.)

Having this appreciation for that little child, I held her as if she were a delicate piece of crystal. On the day of discharge I carefully took her from the arms of my wife. The baby girl was so bundled up for the cold that she was not visible as she slept in the baby carrier. I walked with her, being ever so careful to hold the carrier correctly so as not to disturb the sleeping baby. As I stood waiting, the nurse came by and asked for one final look. Proudly, I allowed her to sort through the blankets for a last look at that cute little face. A burst of laughter from the nurse startled me. My confidence and authority as an experienced father were shattered as I looked at the head of the carrier and saw two bootied feet. I had been holding the sleeping girl upside down all that time. The child was still sweetly innocent, but the father stood convicted as a "greenhorn."

There was, as I look back, one threat to the joy of the occasion. On the day we thought we could take her home, we sensed something was wrong. Our feelings were confirmed when the doctor told us that the baby would have to stay at the hospital, but the mother could return home. There was a jaundis condition which was approaching the level requiring a blood transfusion. This was all new to us, and having to leave for home without the child we had possessed for only two or three days left a darkening void. Our prayers and thoughts seemed to center on the welfare of our daughter. I turned to my own father through long-distance phone calls, and received comfort and support that only a father can give. Though the anxiety of new parents ran high, so did faith and parental support from both sides.

Just before the transfusion level was reached, an improvement was noted. A couple more days, and we were informed that we could take the baby home. The threat had been dispelled, and our new family unit was restored.

From our first child we gained the joy of mortal partnership with the divine, and in a time of difficulty had anticipated the longings of eternal union in eons to come.

Our second child would give us insight toward another direction: a stirring of memory from premortal times.

Cherilyn came along about eighteen months later. Having tired of battling with snow, we had moved to Tempe, Arizona, to soak in the sun. We discovered, however, that there were other elements of opposition not connected with the weather. During the week of delivery, several obstacles occurred which made the second addition a memorable occasion. Our car was hit from behind by a woman on drugs. That necessitated a stay in the shop for our only mode of owned transportation. The evening that we were without a car was the special night. Again I received the warning blow in the ribs by an elbow motivated by experience; the baby was coming. Again I surprised my stomach by jumping up before it was ready. My nausea wasn't lessened by prior experience.

I called my mother-in-law and asked if she could get us to the hospital. Her years of calmness helped as we climbed into her car and raced to the hospital at about 2 a.m. In the labor room, Janene's mother and I tried to offer comfort, but one of us was getting sicker by the minute. "I can't let down," I told myself. "I have to make a good impression." But my stomach wouldn't listen. As Janene endured the pains of labor, I stated in tones of strain: "I don't think I can make it." My mother-in-law looked up in surprise and disbelief as I rushed from the labor room.

"He gets sick to his stomach," Janene explained as I slammed the door to the men's room.

"It really isn't my fault," I thought as I relieved my stomach of the prior day's meals. "It's the timing of the babies. Why can't they come in the daytime?"

I weakly returned to the side of my wife to offer what comfort was left. My mother-in-law said nothing, for which I was grateful.

The moment arrived, and we left for the waiting room as the nurses wheeled my wife toward the delivery room, this time with the doctor present. Again the miracle of birth took place, and a second daughter was added to our family circle.

While this special week saw an addition to our family membership, it also witnessed a subtraction from our family belongings. I went to check on our newly acquired home (our first one) and found shavings of wood at my feet near the carport door. Someone had broken in and helped themselves to our belongings. The material possessions were gone. But the most valuable of our belongings were still safe: our children.

It was just a few days after the return of my wife and new daughter from the hospital that I was taught one of the most touching lessons of my life.

The car had been repaired, our home straightened around, and we were settled back into the routine of daily living. Janene was singing in the kitchen as she prepared the evening meal. I had some moments of rest, so I decided to go into the bedroom and pick up the newest child. I carried her up the hallway. As I entered the living room I raised her above my head with the intent of "joggling" her. It never occurred. As I looked up into her face, her eyes focused upon mine. (I had been told that experts say the eyes of a baby that young don't focus; but I knew what I saw.) Time froze. From the eyes of a child came a message from the spirit inhabiting the newly formed body. A feeling passed from her to me that said: "Here I am." Then there was a pause. Next she seemed to transmit "I'm so happy and excited to be here." I stood as if transfigured, in awe at what was happening. Again, it was as if she were waiting for a response; then after a moment the next message was a question: "Don't you remember?"

My response came without thought. I was so moved that I verbally responded "Yes, I remember."

At that moment the focus and excitement of her eyes disappeared and she became a baby again. I drew her into my arms and sat down to ponder the experience. The communication was so real, the message as clear as any could be. I asked myself, "Why did I respond? I don't remember anything from the premortal existence." Though I had no specific memories, the veil had been thinned enough to cause me to know that somehow this little girl and I had enjoyed an association together before coming to this earth. I sensed that we had an agreement, and this occurrence was in fulfillment of at least a portion of that agreement. I looked again at the baby. The moment had passed, and now the veil of mortality covered the ability of pre-mortal memory; at least, the ability to further communicate that memory.

The evening passed but the message lingered. I shared it with my wife. We knelt in prayer that night with the assurance that permanency was possible. This time I felt that we were not receiving a lease option, but an ownership contract for both of our children. I now felt comfortable in referring to our children as "ours," though I knew that the conditions of ownership must constantly be met and maintained.

Now we had two children with a difference in age of about eighteen months. The question arose "Should all people under any circumstance have all of the children they possibly can as fast as they can?" This was a delicate area, for the counsel is to multiply and replenish the earth. On the other hand, I had watched as an occasional young married sister had so many little children so soon that the health of the mother was adversely affected. One sister almost had a mental breakdown and had to leave the home and family awhile for recovery. Just how does one decide?

My wife and I had a beautiful experience in determining to have children. When we were married, I was still in college with a year of study remaining. We had received opinions from some that we should wait for graduation before deciding to have children. This was, of course, against the counsel of the general authorities. The decision had to be made by us, and it came very naturally.

The scriptures counsel, "Ask, and it shall be given you; seek, and ye shall find; knock, and it shall be opened to you:

"For every one that asketh receiveth; and he that seeketh findeth; and to him that knocketh it shall be opened." (Matthew 7:7-8.)

From the Book of Mormon came the lesson that ". . . The Holy Ghost . . . will show unto you all things what ye should do." (2 Nephi 32:5.)

Since the worth of souls is great in the sight of God, and since having children is such an important matter, it did not seem unreasonable to assume that the Lord would direct by inspiration the parents who sought Him in prayer. Janene and I both felt that we should begin a family right away. We prayed about it individually and together. The witness was of sufficient strength that we both knew that it was right to begin our family. We responded, and it was not long afterward that our first child was on her way.

The same process of inspiration occurred for the second child. We both felt that it was time again, and the second child was soon on its way. We trusted Heavenly Father to be our guide and director in the important matter of having children. He knew what was best. Our challenge was to be in tune enough to receive an answer to our prayers.

We felt that if a couple received the inspiration to begin a family but did not follow through, they placed themselves in critical circumstances. "But ye are commanded in all things to ask of God, who giveth liberally; and that which the Spirit testifies unto you even so I would that ye should do in all holiness of heart, walking uprightly before me . . ." (D&C 46:7.) Had we not followed through with the inspiration we received, I am sure we would have had regrets the rest of our lives.

Time passed. Through prayer and seeking to live the gospel, we again felt that there was another spirit waiting. We responded, and our third child entered the world. There were only minor difficulties in the surroundings this time: we were in the process of moving from our house and the hospital was in the process of moving the baby department.

By experience we knew that when my wife reached a certain point in the labor stage, the next stages went unusually fast. We always seemed to have trouble convincing the nurses of that fact. Their experience indicated a universal element of time they felt they could sense; we seemed to set new records. When that point in time was reached, the nurses again rushed to notify the doctor. When it became apparent that our doctor might not make it, the resident physician was summoned and he prepared for the delivery. Fortunately, our own doctor arrived in time to deliver the baby; but he had to work in his street clothes. Given time to wash his hands and run into the delivery room, he was able to catch the head of the new child as the other physician stepped aside. (It was almost like a touch down pass in the end zone.)

Before I was notified of the delivery, I sensed that this was a child of a noble species. It had not aroused me and my stomach in the "wee" hours of the morning. We had been alerted and sent to the hospital early in the evening, and we were done before midnight. This suited my liking very much. It didn't surprise me, then, to learn that the third one was a boy. Girls were always late, I figured. Maybe the other two were scheduled for a pre-midnight delivery also, but they probably had to stop somewhere along the way to fix their hair or something.

The question of a name is always an exciting challenge. Parents seem to have their own systems. We started out with the first child by picking a name we both thought was pretty. That was the only criteria. We picked "Charlene." Some relatives said that there were no "Charlenes" in the family history, and it would be hard to shorten the name to a nickname. But we ignored the arguments and selected the name we felt best about. The second girl came along and we selected the name of "Cherilyn." This name sounded pretty, also. Then we noticed it started with a "C" like the name of the first child. That started a system. The names of the children would begin with the letter "C." One could ask: "What's so significant about the letter 'C'?" I could answer "It stands for the celestial kingdom!" However, in spite of the nice association, it wasn't so; it just happened that way.

Now we had a boy. "Charlie" was a possibility, but while it was a good name, it didn't settle with us. With this child I was impressed with the concept of heritage and family lineage. While that hadn't been a consideration for the name selection with the girls, we seemed impressed that it should be so with this boy. We selected the name "Carl," the name of my father's father. That name settled with both of us. His middle name became "Brent," the same as his dad.

About three years later, we again felt that there was someone waiting to join our family. We were right, for the fourth child was soon on its way. Having the system down pat, we watched all of the signs during the final hours of waiting and determined when it was time to go to the hospital. This was the first time that we arrived too early. A quick check and we were sent home to wait.

When the time did arrive, we were admitted to the hospital in Salt Lake City, Utah. This was to be the first opportunity I had been given to actually watch the birth of the baby. Everything was set just right. The doctor had been clued in on the speed of delivery, and was expecting the call. I had been "prepped" regarding the clothing I was to wear in the delivery room, and I had the system down perfect. Then it happened.

"It's coming," Janene announced. (She generally knew what she was talking about in that field.) The doctor was summoned—at least the nurses tried. It seemed that there had been a problem in communication and no one could locate our doctor (who unbeknown to any of us was only about two or three blocks away from the hospital).

As with the third child, a resident doctor was called. He cooly walked in to check the stage of labor. In about two seconds he yelled "Get her in there fast!'' As she was rushed out, my calmness left with her.

"You'll have to hurry fast," the nurse warned me as she hurried out the door.

I ran to the change room. I threw on the robe. Then I couldn't find the slippers. When I finally located them and began looking for the next items, I couldn't tell the difference between the caps and the masks. In desparation I put what I thought was a cap on my head and tied a mask on "kitty-corner" with two strings dangling loose as I rushed to the delivery room. Before entering, I heard the cry of the baby. Sure enough, I had missed it.

The nurse looked at me, stiffled a chuckle, explained that I had just missed the birth, and then helped me straighten my clothing around to the point that I looked like I was supposed to be there. Shortly thereafter the doctor rushed in, and I later felt a little sorry for the nurses who caught the brunt of the blame for his missing of the delivery.

I was so thankful Janene and the new baby girl were all right that I held no bad feelings. Being even that close to the birth process was a real thrill for me.

The name, of course, had to start with the letter "C." Who could break tradition at this point? "Cathryn" was selected.

The special lesson we gained from her was a renewal of love, patience, and sweetness from a precious little girl with a bright smile and an inborn sense of self-worth. All of the family turned to her with feelings of joy and love.

Time moved along as it always does, except that it seemed to speed up a little. The innocence of babyhood melted away as the children grew and became more independent. By the time we had met the challenges of a baby, it was a toddler. When we caught up to the toddler stage, the boy or girl had moved ahead of us again with new challenges and joys. I found that it was a lot of hard work to try to rear a family correctly, especially when each member had an individual will. I never doubted the inspiration in having the children, but I sometimes joked that we had three children more than we could afford and four more than I knew how to rear properly. On one of my dad's visits, he dropped a bit of wisdom from his father that I immediately adopted: "I wouldn't take a million dollars for any of my children—but I wouldn't give a nickel for another one."

I had often wondered about the family organization in the pre-mortal existence. From my experience with Cherilyn, I knew that at least some of the time there were pre-mortal ties. I began to wonder if we were really through with our family; so did my wife. This time she relied on my inspiration, and I wanted to be sure. Perhaps I resisted a little the feelings I had. I thought we had all we could handle and couldn't afford another child. Yet I didn't want to deny the privilege of birth to someone if there were more to come. It was a frustrating struggle. I wanted an answer, but was afraid of the possibilities. The answer came one evening in the form of a dream. I sensed that I was walking hurriedly to get to a business appointment of some sort. As I walked along, I heard the crying of a small child. I looked to my right and saw a single panel of bars (like in a jail) with a small child in a white robe standing at the bars, head down, crying. My first inclination was to hurry past and get to my appointment, assuming that someone else would find time to help the child. But for some reason, I turned against logic and reached for the bars. There was no visible lock. When I took hold of one of the bars, the gate swung open and I picked up the child. I hugged it close and offered comfort. As the crying began to subside, I awoke from my dream. Though symbolic in nature, I was certain that my prayers had been answered.

After a miscarriage and a little recovery time, Janene was expecting our fifth child. We were happy, yet concerned as to whether or not the new one would fit into the family constellation without arousing feelings of jealousy or antagonism because of less room in the home for the others. We wanted the children to wholeheartedly accept the new one. We prayed, and hoped.

The day of delivery drew nigh. It was summer. I was involved in a stake musical. The cast prayed that the child would come safely—but not during a performance. The first show was to be on the twenty-fourth of July. On the twenty-third, I rehearsed on stage while my wife timed labor pains at home. Between the final rehearsal and the opening performance it happened.

Off to the hospital we rushed in the early hours of morning. With warning lights blinking, I pretended to be an ambulance driver as we moved through the empty streets. After having practiced with four other deliveries, we finally got everything right. We were neither too early nor too late. The doctor was there ahead of time and visited until the delivery. I was properly dressed and in place when the moment of birth arrived. I saw the miracle as it occurred and was so enthralled that the doctor had to ask, "Well, aren't you going to take any pictures?"

About the only thing that really caught us off guard was the selection of an appropriate name. We had sorted through several girls' names and had centered on the one we liked best. The baby turned out to be a boy. Rather than doing our homework all over again, we looked at the little guy and said "He looks like a Curtis." And so it would be: Curtis (for the "C") Grant (after a grandfather) and Farley.

When we brought this one home, all of the fears of jealousy or inconvenience were totally unfounded. Instead of leaving the feeling of "crowding in," Curtis brought such a unity of love and concern from the other children that we've often wondered if our family would have survived without him.

Somewhere along the way the concept of "leasing" had given way to "owning." Perhaps the attempt to follow the counsel in D&C 68:25-28 aided in the process. Prayers, counsel from family members, lessons in church organizations, and service at home guided by gospel standards built our family unit. Though we had our problems, we had our joys and we now look forward with the hope that the principle of ownership will be our reward throughout time and into the eternities.

In our early parenthood, we sensed that the children came on a lease arrangement (for mortality) with the option to "buy" (for immortality). The price is good parenting, according to ability, within the framework of the restored gospel. If bought (symbolically), children become "pearls of great price." With these pearls we gain entrance into the kingdom of heaven. Thus an investment becomes a fortune and brings the returns of joy which we yet hope to gain as we continue our efforts toward ownership.

CHAPTER EIGHT

Child Rearing Guides From The Creation Account

Did you ever notice the implications for the successful rearing of children contained within the story of the creation?

As I read the creation account in the books of Moses and Abraham, I was intrigued to discover many parenting ideas hidden within the context of the story. There was a surprising amount of material available. While much of the information was not primarily directed toward parenting, inference and application were surprisingly apt. Here are some of the items I gleaned.

"And it came to pass that the Lord spake unto Moses, saying: Behold, I reveal unto you concerning this heaven, and this earth; write the words which I speak. I am the Beginning and the End, the Almighty God; by mine Only Begotten I created these things . . ." (Moses 2:1.) After introducing Himself, the story centers upon His work in creating for the benefit of mankind. In fact, that is the work and glory of God, to bring to pass the eternal life of man (Moses 1:39). If preparing for and working with children is of such a major and central theme in the role of God, this would indicate that the major and central theme in the development of men and women are their preparations for children and the resultant work in rearing them properly. This suggests that a person will never be as fulfilled with the single life, or married childless life (by choice), as with marriage and children. These are irreplaceable in the happiness and satisfaction of men and women.

Abraham 4:1 begins: "Let us . . ." The word "us" is important. It may be applied in our analogy to the joint effort of both father and mother in rearing children. It is not an "I" or a "me" situation. "We" are important when it comes to parenting. No distinction of importance is allowed for any one person in the process. While the mother may be closer to the children in early stages of growth, yet she does not hold precedence over the father in net effect of influence upon the children. When the father plays a key role in the life of a son or daughter, he does not take preeminence over the mother, or cancel out her early effect upon the child.

The scripture continues with ". . . go down." How appropriate a hint for the teaching of children. First of all, go down to the level of their interest and understanding. Young children may not get much from a lecture in home evening on "let your light shine." But turn off the lights and light a candle in preparation for the message. They'll not forget it quickly. The perusal of books designed for the age or grade level of the children in your family will give clues to the parents about the level of vocabulary and understanding to be met, as well as their attention span.

Going down also implies that parents ought to find out what's important to the child. This opens up the field for effective communication and teaching, for we have stepped out of our realm and into the world of the child. Spelling, sports, questions about God, fairness, equal turns, the purpose of a bug, why hands need to be washed . . . parents know how the list extends.

Another help. Parents loom above children by several feet. Kneeling down to meet the eye level of the child may help, in a casual moment, to teach or discuss without the threatening dominion of authority, or strength through difference of size. A child on a lap may be more responsive at eye level than the mother looking down at the toddler.

One other point comes to mind in the "going down" concept. Children today are often not allowed to be children. They are rushed by adults into a grown-up set of values and competition. Early sports competition coached and cheered by the parents, elementary girls dressed in cheerleading outfits, emphasis on clothes and styles, winning and standing out, pairing off of boys and girls in social settings, etc., tends to place demands and expectancies upon the children that they would not otherwise approach in the course of their own normal development. It seems sometimes that children can't just be kids, and play in the sandbox, or make mud pies, or choose what they want to do. Going down would imply that the child's developmental interests ought not to be "jerked up" to the interest levels of the adults. Adulthood can be acquired in the normal course of events without the interference of a fast-paced society of parents.

In the scriptural account they went down ". . . at the beginning . . ." When is the beginning in the preparation of a child? In the written scriptural record, man was not yet on the scene. They were preparing before the mortal birth of human beings. Would not the proper preparation for children begin before birth? The mother who smokes, takes drugs, or violates the laws of health and nutrition runs a high risk of adversely affecting the child not yet born. Mental and emotional preparation are assets the future mother or father ought to acquire long before the birth of any children.

What about the fun of planning the furniture, clothing, names, etc? There is much to do before the child enters the scene.

Then the Gods ". . . organized and formed the heavens and the earth." You, as expectant parents, are organizing and forming a mortal body for a spirit who already exists with emotion, personality, and a certain degree of progress based upon experience and the use of free agency.

Moses 2:2 states that ". . . the earth was without form, and void . . ." Is this similar to the shock of being born? An adult spirit is placed in a child's body without means of travel or open communication. What perspective does the baby have with regard to the world?

Abraham 4:3 says, "And they (the Gods) said: Let there be light . . ." Light implies good. Standards and conditions can be declared and provided so that the world of the child is illuminated with opportunities for good. The parents won't be fighting, nor will the brothers and sisters. The home will have a good feeling or atmosphere within it. It's degree of cleanliness will be an asset rather than a liability. The music, TV programs, and magazines found within the home will be complimentary to gospel standards. The programs of the church, such as home evening and family prayers, will be followed.

In the next verses it states that ". . . they (the Gods) comprehended the light . . ." The parents ought to comprehend the light. They should follow church guidelines within the home, not just because it is the program, but because they know it is right. A testimony of the program is needed, with an understanding of the end results possible for the children.

Then it states ". . . they divided the light, or caused it to be divided, from the darkness." Parents too must divide the light from the darkness, the good from the bad. They must know the difference clearly if they are to teach it to the children. They must "call it like it is." If something is bad, the parents need the wisdom to label it bad so the child need not wrestle with the decision. Insecurity is the byproduct of unclear value selection. As much good as possible must be brought into the home, and as much bad as possible kept out. Parents must know the difference and understand not only the value of the good but the threat of the bad. A clear-cut differentiation is a valuable asset in the life of a child.

"And the Gods called the light Day, and the darkness they called Night." (Abraham 4:5.) The decision was made: they stated it. Could this suggest to parents of young children that they should make the early decisions? When the decisions are beyond the capability of the child, the wise parent can take over. This may mean stating that the children will eat balanced meals and not junk foods, that they will go to bed at a certain time, take naps, stay out of the street, etc. As the child matures, he might then take over these decisions.

In Moses 2:6-13, the creation continues by degrees. Parents create environments by degrees for their children in order to stimulate proper development. This is noted in the expansion of the child's world from the crib to the house, the yard, and eventually the neighborhood. The same advancement is noted in the foods that the child handles from baby stage to childhood; also the level of responsibility entrusted to a youngster.

The key in creating an environment is to provide the materials that the child will need at any particular level of development, plus a stimulus to use those materials and improve.

In Abraham 4:8 the expanse is called "heaven," and in verse 10 the dry land is called "earth." A child needs both a "heaven" and an "earth" setting, ·the mortal and the spiritual. He needs the food and clothing, the sandpile and lawn, the bathing and sleeping. The heavenly part could be the love and warmth, the prayers and home evenings, and the expressions of faith and testimony from family members. The two areas compliment each other rather than conflict, though there may be times when one element needs emphasis over the other for a particular purpose.

In Abraham 4:9, the Gods "ordered." This may be the justification some parents have been looking for. There are times in the life of a child, and even a youth, when it is appropriate for parents to issue an order. Some things have to be stated and carried out under the direction of the parents. "You cannot go to the overnight party." "Your room must be cleaned before the company arrives." "You have to eat a balanced meal." When there is a standard that is good and the child hasn't the maturity to select it, parents may appropriately declare that standard on the authority that it is right. This is more successful with younger children, but possible at times with older youth.

Abraham 4:11 states: "Let us prepare the earth to bring forth . . ." Parents can prepare environments for their children which will be conducive to growth and development. Trips, hobbies, music, play areas in the yard, educational toys, etc., can stimulate development without force. Children will be motivated by the things around them, and parents can do something to make those things interesting and educational.

Continuing through verse 11 and into verse 12, the environment is set in such a manner that planted seeds will bring forth after their own kinds. Many seeds are planted in the home, both knowingly and unknowingly, by the parents. Those seeds will bring forth after their own kinds. If disharmony and anger are found in the home, the child will likely have those seeds reproduced in his own life. If love and trust are planted, these will reproduce. Parents ought to take stock and determine what types of seeds they are planting in the lives of their children. Children will imitate such virtues as kindness, love, honor, prayers, reading, home evening involvement, payment of tithes, settling of differences without anger, etc. If seeds are sown, these activities and qualities will continue without the immediate supervision of the parents. The ways a parent reacts in times of stress will likely be acquired by the children, so seeds of maturity are especially valuable here.

Abraham 4:14-17 describes the plans for the organization of lights, two of them being greater. Forgetting the notable difference between sun and moon, the two greater lights might represent the mother and father. They could also represent Heavenly Father and Jesus.

There will be many other lights in the life of the child, just as there are many other lights in the heavens. Teachers and leaders in primary, Sunday school, scouting, MIA, school, etc., will provide light and direction for the children as they grow. Think back through your own lifetime. Are there any teachers or other individuals who come quickly to your mind who made good impressions upon you when you needed help? What about the ones who don't come readily to mind? Were they any less significant? Who can count the contributions all these lights make to our lives?

There are also implications for the selection of friends within these scriptures. How many of one's associates could be classed with the category of "light"? Should one settle for less light than is available?

In Abraham 4:20-25, the earth and the waters bring forth creatures. What do creatures have to do with the child? They were designed as benefits to the environment, and for the edification of man. Could this suggest a value in pets for the children at appropriate stages? Dogs, cats, fish, etc., can enrich the lives of children and give them opportunities for growth, intellectually and emotionally. We currently have nine birds (all with personal names and individual personalities), a mommie and daddy hampster with eight babies, two rabbits, two mice, and a dog named "Peaches." They provide moments of fun, intrigue, adventure, education, glee, and other moments I wouldn't care to mention.

In Abraham 4:26 ". . . the Gods took counsel among themselves . . ." How many times does a child ask dad about something and his response is "Go ask your mother?"

"But I just did and she said to ask you."

"Then we'll talk it over and decide," dad might say. Then dad and mom take counsel among themselves to unite on a decision. Having a family council is also good in making decisions.

In verse 26, plans are made to give man "dominion." This is especially important in the life of a child. He needs dominion over something all of the time. It could be a special toy, blanket, room, bed, pet, etc. Something must be his that he can own and have dominion over, without the fear of losing it through interference of parents, brothers and sisters, friends, etc.

This need extends throughout one's lifetime. Perhaps that is why the principle was declared in the beginning by a wise Heavenly Father.

Abraham 4:27 states, "So the Gods went down to organize man in their own image, in the image of the Gods to form they him, male and female to form they them." As parents we pick up that commission, or goal: to guide our children in the direction of conforming to the image of godhood. "And Jesus increased in wisdom and stature, and in favour with God and man." (Luke 2:52.) There is a model for the rearing of children.

Abraham 4:28 gives the directive "We will bless them." There are priesthood blessings that ought to be given in the homes of the saints. Birthdays, other special events, times of stress and illness, etc., are some of the times that a father ought to extend blessings to his children. Where a father is not present, home teachers or family members holding the priesthood could fill that void.

The next verse says, "Behold, we will give them every herb . . . and every tree which shall have fruit . . . for their meat." Parents freely provide the food and lodging for children with no thoughts of reimbursement or future gain. I once knew a high school student who was required to pay his mother a monthly salary to clean his room and provide his meals. Needless to say, he suffered a deep sense of insecurity and a loss of self-respect.

Abraham 4:31 is interesting when applied to modern parents. It provides a hint of optimism, sometimes unexperienced optimism as used by novice parents. After stating that "We will do everything that we have said," indicating that good parental plans are of little value unless carried out, it continues ". . . and behold, they shall be very obedient." There's an idealistic goal for parents. Obedience is a great virtue in children, and a quality that parents would wisely hope for.

In Moses 3:2, God ended His work and "rested" on the seventh day. Parents literally need an occasional rest, or break, from the routine of rearing children. An evening or weekend together for just mom and dad can do wonders in rejuvenation. The parents need attention and self-care, too.

Perhaps the seventh day, the Sabbath, comes as the child matures and gives his first talk in Sunday School, bears his testimony, makes a right decision on his own, goes on a mission, marries in the temple, rears children of his own, etc. The final Sabbath would occur when the parent sees the child obtain the greatest gift available: eternal life.

In Moses 3:9, it indicates that the environment ". . . is pleasant to the sight of man. . . ." Parents ought to keep a pleasant environment for their children. This indicates a clean and attractive home or apartment, a nice yard (if available), plants, pictures, and other items that add optical beauty to the environment.

An important lesson is given in Moses 3:15 for children. "And I, the Lord God, took the man, and put him into the Garden of Eden, to dress it, and to keep it." Man had a responsibility in the care of his environment. Children ought to be commissioned to care for something, such as their rooms, specific areas of household chores, a portion of the yard work, or other duties deemed appropriate by the parents. This responsibility provides important lessons in work, accountability, and self-esteem. It communicates trust from the parents to the children.

In Moses 3:16-17, the Lord gives a commandment. He also allows free agency, and explains the consequences if a choice is made contrary to the commandment. As a child matures, parents can give commandments of right, point out the consequences of violation of those principles, and make allowance for free agency. This is particularly valuable for the teen-age years when children sense their free agency and rights of choice. If one is not willing to keep the commandment (or direction) of a good principle, he ought to know the consequences of a wrong choice and understand that he is accountable for the decision. If a parent cannot direct the course of an older child, he ought to at least recommend the best route if the youth is willing to listen.

Abraham 5:14 indicates that ". . . It is not good that the man should be alone, . . ." Thus, a helpmeet is given. It is not good for children to be alone. Someone close to his own stage of development, who can provide friendship and association, is a valuable asset. A brother, sister, or friend can fill the need. Total aloneness is not good for anyone.

A growing child, left to the public or private nurseries while both parents work, will sense a feeling of aloneness even though surrounded by peers.

Moses 3:24 indicates that the man will leave father and mother and ". . . cleave unto his wife; . . ." The children will mature and eventually leave to build homes of their own. Parents can prepare their children for an easy but loving departure. No child should feel guilty for leaving, nor should apron strings be so tight that it is a traumatic experience to leave home for a worthy purpose. Parents need to realize the cycle of progress does not remain static and immobile. If we had feared to leave the presence of our parents in the premortal existence, none of us would be here now. We would not have the opportunity for advancement and would forfeit the happiness of a celestial life in postmortal existence. The parents' work and glory could well emulate the Father's in bringing to pass the stability and future happy lives of their children. A celestial reunion will culminate the cycle of progress and bring parents and children together again eternally.

The early portions of the story in the Pearl of Great Price record God's preparation and doings for man; later in the story the focus shifts to man's doings to draw closer to or further away from God. Applied to our own lives, the early stages of childhood are the formative years where parents can perhaps do the most to insure good lives for their children. As the children grow, they take more and more responsibility and freedom in their lives and the focus of accountability centers on them more than their parents.

While it is not good to stretch the meanings of the scriptures beyond intent, it is interesting to pick up some implications from the account of the preparation of the earth by a perfect Father for His children. There could be many other applications a reader could find. These were some of the interesting parallels I found as I read, as a parent, the account of another parent's preparations and dealings with His children.

CHAPTER NINE

The Truth Shall Make You Free

Joseph Smith listened to what Pilate would not wait to hear: the answer to the question "What is truth?"

"And truth is knowledge of things as they are, and as they were, and as they are to come." (D&C 93:24.)

Within that concise definition is housed the beautiful purpose of existence. Man alone could never have devised so comprehensive a definition.

Truth consists of knowledge. Knowledge is built as one perceives, discovers, and acquires information. The information of most worth is not the superficial material of existence and entertainment such as where we live, where a movie is playing, how much gas is in the car, etc. The knowledge of most worth has to do with the gospel plan. While knowledge of temporal affairs may be gained in school, knowledge of spiritual affairs is obtained only by those who qualify for higher learning.

Alma gave a masterful discourse for the process of gaining this higher level knowledge in Alma 32. He denotes a hierarchy leading to perfect knowledge. The upper levels of the hierarchy seem to grow out of the condition of humility and repentance (Alma 32:12-16). Then by allowing place for a true seed to be planted, and by nourishing that seed, a knowledge of its truthfulness can be obtained.

As a young man, I listened to others bear their testimonies of the gospel. I wondered how they could know the gospel was true. I felt that they knew something of value that I did not know, and I wanted to gain such knowledge. A hope was planted in my mind and heart. Nourishment of that hope led to such a powerful witness from the Spirit that my belief was transformed into knowledge. I, too, could then bear witness that I knew the gospel was true.

If the seed being investigated is not good, Alma explained that it will not grow, or produce any feelings of goodness, enlargement, or enlightenment. It is therefore to be discarded (Alma 32:32) since it will not lead one to God, the source of all goodness (Moroni 7:24).

There are philosophers who challenge the credibility of knowledge or experiences of this nature that are not open to the general public. Religious experiences imparting knowledge to certain individuals may be looked upon with scorn and scepticism. The point they seem to miss is that as there is a hierarchy of temporal knowledge, the bottom level of which is open to all individuals and the top of which is attained by only the diligent and studious; so it is with spiritual knowledge. Every person has a conscience as a guide, but only the diligent attain higher levels of witnesses regarding spiritual truth.

Truth, then, consists of knowledge, and knowledge can be verified by the Spirit.

What then are we to obtain knowledge of? In the definition of truth it begins to answer by listing ". . . things as they are . . ." One might ask, "How are things?"

The answer is gained from scripture. "We will make an earth whereon these may dwell;

"And we will prove them herewith, to see if they will do all things whatsoever the Lord their God shall command them." (Abraham 3:24-25.)

Things as they presently are may not be correctly perceived or stated by philosophers, psychologists, or sociological experts. The proper view of things as they are is gained from an eternal perspective, as revealed from a being who has a perfect knowledge and who is willing to share that knowledge. That individual, God, shared the knowledge that things are here for a purpose and that human beings are being tested. Whatever they do, think, say, believe, etc., all relate to the test they are undergoing ". . . to see if they will do all things whatsoever the Lord their God shall command them."

Things as they are, then, include the test of mortality and everything associated with the environment in which one is being tested, whether or not perceived by the one undergoing the test.

What else is real in the context of "things as they are?" Good and evil. These constitute the opposing elements of the test. The sources of these qualities are traceable:

"Wherefore, all things which are good cometh of God; and that which is evil cometh of the devil; for the devil is an enemy unto God, and fighteth against him continually, and inviteth and enticeth to sin, and to do that which is evil continually." (Moroni 7:12.)

"And that wicked one [Satan] cometh and taketh away light and truth, through disobedience, from the children of men." (D&C 93:39.)

"But behold, that which is of God inviteth and enticeth to do good continually; wherefore, every thing which inviteth and enticeth to do good, and to love God, and to serve him, is inspired of God." (Moroni 7:13.)

The contrast between these opposing forces was heightened for me through my association with a young man I shall call Hank. My first contact with Hank came at 1:30 a.m. as the phone aroused me from sleep. When I answered, Hank identified himself as a member of our ward (I was serving as the second counselor in the bishopric; the bishop and the first counselor were out of town). He then began to slur his words together so rapidly that I couldn't understand what he was saying. After repeating the message again, I got him to slow down enough to clarify his speech. I picked out that he was having problems with evil spirits, was at a street corner near Arizona State University, and he wanted me to pick him up. I got the address, then said I'd be right down. Being young, naive, and anxious to help, I quickly got dressed and drove off in the night to find a ward member I did not know who was having trouble with evil spirits. (I vowed after the experience that although things worked out all right and I was protected, I would thereafter take another priesthood holder with me on such occasions.)

I found Hank and his friend on the designated corner, picked them up, dropped his friend off at the home of another church member, and took Hank to our home.

Hank was visibly nervous, and when invited to sleep on the couch refused, asking if he might sit up the remainder of the night with the light on. He also requested a Book of Mormon to read.

When dawn arrived, Hank was more settled and I visited with him. He was a large individual doing graduate work at A.S.U. He indicated that he had done some things consistently in his life that were not in harmony with gospel standards, yet none of the questionable items were within the category of sin that would require a church court on any single account. He had, in effect, been living on the "edge" of the line of safety. In doing so, he had discovered that Satan had a difficult hold to break, even though he felt he had only "strayed a little."

The coming weeks included interviews between Hank and the bishop, a psychiatrist, and me and the other counselor in the bishopric, Richard Jacobs. Rich and I knelt with Hank as he prayed for strength. He would weep and cry in a high falsetto voice, "Please, Heavenly Father, help me to get out of this difficulty, please, please," repeated over and over again. "Please don't let Satan get me," he would cry, shaking as he prayed.

We watched Hank try to cast evil spirits out of his apartment one day. He held the Melchizedek Priesthood, said all the right words, but nothing happened. When a counselor repeated the process, the evil left.

Hank continued to struggle with his life, and eventually did face a church court and disciplinary action. I lost track of him after completing my degree and moving to another ward.

About two years later I again received a call from Hank. He was excited to share with me the news that he had been reinstated in the church and had received his first church calling to serve in the MIA. I, too, was excited with the news, for it seemed that hell had been robbed of Hank. The unhappy portion of the story is that his difficulties cost him the companionship and love of his wife and children. Hank knew, by firsthand experience, the contrast between good and evil in "things as they are."

The plan designed to bring one successfully through the testing experience of mortality is called the gospel.

"And this is my gospel—repentance and baptism by water, and then cometh the baptism of fire and the Holy Ghost, even the Comforter, which showeth all things, and teacheth the peaceable things of the kingdom." (D&C 39:6.)

Concisely, then, things as they are include people, the environment in which they live, the test they undergo, the elements comprising the opposing forces of good and evil, and the sources of these elements.

The definition of truth continues with "Truth is knowledge of things as they are, and as they were."

The next question is, "How were things?"

Joseph Fielding Smith gave some pertinent explanations of things as they were when he explained that all human beings existed as spirits (human form, but lacking physical bodies) before coming to this earth. These spirits were children of God, our Heavenly Father, and lived with and were educated by Him. Mortal life was desired by these spirits in order to achieve two vital purposes: the gaining of a mortal body and the opportunity to have experience that could not be obtained anywhere else.

Councils were held where decisions vital to mortality were made. Schooling was conducted to prepare individuals for that mortality. The gospel was taught, and spirits had free agency to accept it and to progress in knowledge and experience. Some individuals progressed further than others, and this progress had a direct bearing on each one's mortality: place of birth, nationality, disposition, etc. The memories of this existence were covered at birth so that each person might be tested independent of prior knowledge to see which force they would tend to follow. However, dispositions and abilities were not removed, but the memory of premortality was dimmed out. Thus, some individuals were assigned to accomplish certain tasks to further the cause of humanity upon the earth, assuming they remained faithful and sought out sufficient knowledge of a higher level to activate them in their potentials. Free agency was to be respected in the mortal estate just as it was in the premortal.*

Referring to the Pearl of Great Price, "We will make an earth whereon these may dwell;

"And we will prove them herewith, to see if they will do all things whatsoever the Lord their God shall command them;

"And they who keep their first estate shall be added upon; and they who keep not their first estate shall not have glory in the same kingdom with those who keep their first estate." (Abraham 3:24-26.)

The first estate mentioned is the premortal existence. The reference to some not keeping that first estate accounts for the existence of Satan (and his angels). The principle of free agency and choice allowed for differences there, some of which led to a great premortal conflict.

"And there was war in heaven: Michael and his angels fought against the dragon; and the dragon fought and his angels,

"And prevailed not; neither was their place found any more in heaven.

"And the great dragon was cast out, that old serpent, called the Devil, and Satan, which deceiveth the whole world: he was cast out into the earth, and his angels were cast out with him." (Revelation 12:7-9.)

These individuals, by the misuse of their agency, forfeited the right to continue on to the second estate to gain a mortal body and enter into the test. Thus the devil is more than a myth; he is a reality. So is his work. Satan provides the source of evil in the test and quest for a knowledge of existence and its components.

"And thus he has laid a cunning plan, thinking to destroy the work of God; . . .

"Yea, he stirreth up their hearts to anger against this work.

"Yea, he saith unto them: Deceive and lie in wait to catch, that ye may destroy; behold, this is no harm. And thus he flattereth them, and telleth them that it is no sin to lie that they may catch a man in a lie, that they may destroy him.

"And thus he flattereth them, and leadeth them along until he draggeth their souls down to hell; and thus he causeth them to catch themselves in their own snare.

"And thus he goeth up and down, to and fro in the earth, seeking to destroy the souls of men." (D&C 10:23-27.)

All of this coming from "things as they were" to "things as they are."

Counterbalancing the forces of Satan, "The Lord had shown unto me, Abraham, the intelligences that were organized before the world was; and among all these there were many of the noble and great ones;

---

*See Joseph Fielding Smith, *Doctrines of Salvation,* 1:56-61, 66.

"And God saw these souls that they were good, and he stood in the midst of them, and he said: These I will make my rulers; for he stood among those that were spirits, and he saw that they were good." (Abraham 3:22-23.)

Those who thus excelled were ". . . called and prepared from the foundation of the world according to the foreknowledge of God, on account of their exceeding faith and good works; in the first place being left to choose good or evil; therefore they having chosen good, and exercising exceeding great faith, are called with a holy calling, yea, with that holy calling which was prepared with, and according to, a preparatory redemption for such.

"And thus they have been called to this holy calling on account of their faith, while others would reject the Spirit of God on account of the hardness of their hearts and blindness of their minds, while, if it had not been for this they might have had as great privilege as their brethren." (Alma 13:3-4.)

At the head of these great individuals was the greatest of all, Jesus, the one chosen to be the Savior.

Thus the two forces with their proponents and the great preparation scenes for mortality came into being in the period referred to as ". . . things as they were."

Remaining in the definition of truth is the reference to ". . . things . . . as they are to come." (D&C 93:24.) The question: How will things be?

Referring back to Abraham 3:26 and continuing, "And they who keep their second estate shall have glory added upon their heads for ever and ever."

To make a determination of who is worthy for such an inheritance in the world to come, an evaluation will be conducted at the conclusion of the testing experiences of mortal life. Said John, in vision of future events:

"And I saw the dead, small and great, stand before God; and the books were opened: and another book was opened, which is the book of life: and the dead were judged out of those things which were written in the books, according to their works." (Revelation 20:12.)

The first reference to books (records of mortality) could include all those records kept by men in relation to gospel principles and activity of individuals within the gospel (as well as any other mortal records). These records would necessarily have the limitations of mortality inherent in their contents. An additional record, "the book of life," could provide the final perfect elements of a fair judgment for all human beings, as referred to in the Book of Mormon where it is stated: "And behold, all things are written by the Father; therefore out of the books which shall be written shall the world be judged." (3 Nephi 27:25.) How the Father writes and maintains that record is not specified; it is simply stated that it is so.

Since men are leaving mortality at different periods of time, an intermediate residence is prepared between mortal life and one's final place of residence after the judgment. This intermediary residence also follows a pattern of a heirarchy of degrees.

"The spirits of those who are righteous are received into a state of happiness, which is called paradise, a state of rest, a state of peace, where they shall rest from all their troubles and from all care, and sorrow." (Alma 40:12.)

It need not be supposed, however, that such an existence is without work and progress, for the Lord stated in relation to life and death: "If they live here let them live unto me; and if they die let them die unto me; for they shall rest from all their labors here, and shall continue their works." (D&C 124:86.)

Those who are not righteous have a different state to enter.

"The spirits of the wicked, yea, who are evil—for behold, they have no part nor portion of the Spirit of the Lord; for behold, they chose evil works rather than good; therefore the spirit of the devil did enter into them, and take possession of their house—and these shall be cast out into outer darkness; there shall be weeping, and wailing, and gnashing of teeth, and this because of their own iniquity being led captive by the will of the devil." (Alma 40:13.)

These taste the bitterness of hell that is often referred to in the scriptures.

The final state of all individuals, following mortal and spirit world existences, falls within a hierarchy. The Savior said, "In my Father's house are many mansions: if it were not so, I would have told you. I go to prepare a place for you." (John 14:2.) The Father's house consists of the "celestial" kingdom where the most valiant go. The next kingdom lower is named "terrestrial," and the lowest one is named "telestial."

Though he didn't name the telestial kingdom, Paul referred to these kingdoms when he said "There are also celestial bodies, and bodies terrestrial: but the glory of the celestial is one, and the glory of the terrestrial is another.

"There is one glory of the sun, and another glory of the moon, and another glory of the stars: for one star differeth from another star in glory. So also is the resurrection of the dead." (1 Corinthians 15:40-42.)

Joseph Smith provided further details of these kingdoms and who qualifies for each in the Doctrine and Covenants, section 76.

A universal aspect of things as they are to come is the resurrection, mentioned by Paul and other prophets. As the premortal spirit departs from the mortal body in death, so will it return to the body when it is resurrected in immortality.

"The soul shall be restored to the body, and the body to the soul; yea, and every limb and joint shall be restored to its body; yea, even a hair of the head shall not be lost; but all things shall be restored to their proper and perfect frame." (Alma 40:23.)

This all takes place as a result of the mission of the Savior.

So death, intermediate residences, evaluations of mortal tests, resurrections, and assignments of results in the form of final habitations for mankind, all based upon things as they are and were, come about within the context of "things as they are to come."

The definition of truth, then, is a knowledge of things as they were in premortal life, things as they are in mortality, and things as they will be in postmortal life, all based upon an eternal perspective, as revealed by God to those individuals who seek such knowledge.

That definition appears to embody the essential elements of all human existence. It is as if the whole philosophy of Mormonism were clothed in that masterful definition of truth, waiting to be discovered by those who ascend the ladder of knowledge step by step, and who do not fall under the condemnation pronounced by the Savior upon certain individuals when He said:

"By hearing ye shall hear, and shall not understand; and seeing ye shall not perceive: For this people's heart is waxed gross, and their ears are dull of hearing, and their eyes they have closed; lest at any time they should see with their eyes, and hear with their ears, and should understand with their heart, and should be converted." (Matthew 13:15.)

Just as Pilate turned his back and walked away from the one who was able to define truth, so will many today reject him, for ". . . the natural man receiveth not the things of the Spirit of God: for they are foolishness unto him: neither can he know them, because they are spiritually discerned." (1 Corinthians 2:14.)

But for those who wait and listen to the Master, "It is written, Eye hath not seen, nor ear heard, neither have entered into the heart of man, the things which God hath prepared for them that love him.

"But God hath revealed them . . . by his Spirit: for the Spirit searcheth all things, yea, the deep things of God.

"For what man knoweth the things of a man, save the spirit of man which is in him? even so the things of God knoweth no man, but the Spirit of God.

"Now we have received, not the spirit of the world, but the spirit which is of God; that we might know the things that are freely given to us of God.

"Which things also we speak, not in the words which man's wisdom teacheth, but which the Holy Ghost teacheth." (1 Corinthians 2:9-13.)

So truth stands, and man stands or falls by his ability to gain knowledge of that truth.

CHAPTER TEN

The Measure Of Intelligence: "I.Q." Or "C.Q."?

Educators have long sought a reliable method of measuring intelligence. The "intelligence quotient" is one of the more widely known and used labels. It is found by multiplying the mental age by one hundred and dividing by the chronological age. It is a concept which has been questioned as to total accuracy; nevertheless it has been a useful tool.

Is the intelligence quotient the best indicator of intelligence, or is there something more accurate? I would suggest that the Latter-day Saints have the most accurate method of all in measuring intelligence.

How do we establish an indicator of intelligence? First we find a reference point. For Latter-day Saints, that is easy. The perfect example of intelligence is found in the Lord.

"And the Lord said unto me: These two facts do exist, that there are two spirits, one being more intelligent than the other; there shall be another more intelligent than they; I am the Lord thy God, I am more intelligent than they all." (Abraham 3:19.)

In fact, "The glory of God is intelligence, or, in other words, light and truth." (D&C 93:36.)

In the Lord, then, is a perfect example of knowledge and intelligence. Nephi said "O how great the holiness of our God! For he knoweth all things, and there is not anything save he knows it." (2 Nephi 9:20.)

The Lord is not learning and discovering. He knows all that can be known. His progress is not found in the realm of increasing knowledge and intelligence, for He possesses a fulness.

How does that help the Latter-day Saints? They obviously cannot know or comprehend all that God knows, but they can select the perfect reference point of knowledge and intelligence. Then the question follows: "How can we become more intelligent?"

The answer follows: "Become more like God."

How does one do that?

By keeping the commandments. "He that keepeth his commandments receiveth truth and light, until he is glorified in truth and knoweth all things." (D&C 93:28.)

This reasoning is not subject to verification by worldly logic or argument; it is factual. Those who come closest to the Lord will be the more intelligent; those who stray the furtherest will be the less intelligent. The court of human learning is not the trial grounds for eternal truth. Intelligence is established when human wisdom approaches divine parameters.

Not all educators would accept that premise; only the more intelligent ones would.

I recall registering for a philosophy class as a requirement for the master's degree I was pursuing. After signing up for a particular section, I was informed by several Latter-day Saint students that my teacher was anti-religious. His reputation included making laughing stocks out of Latter-day Saint church and educational leaders. Guest Latter-day Saint speakers had been made to appear comical and far from intelligent in front of the college-student audiences of his classes. I was also warned that Mormon students tended to get low grades in his classes; in his view, an obvious mark of lesser intelligence.

I decided to keep the class. I also decided to keep my mouth shut as to religion.

I soon found that what I had heard was true. This professor, though an excellent teacher as to methodology, was a prime example of an anti-Christ. Had he lived in Book of Mormon times, he would probably have made an excellent drinking buddy for Korihor. In fact, Korihor may have come in second to him.

Religion was constantly the target of his jokes and ridicule. Revelation and testimony were classed with mysticism and witchcraft, all of which received a smile of scorn. He became very popular with his students, who soon thrived upon his philosophy of life.

The two or three Mormons were quickly discovered (except me) by the professor. They rose to the baited questions, and he quickly set the hook. Within his terms of intelligence, they were rapidly "put down" in the eyes of their classmates. An attempt to discuss testimony would turn the class toward a humorous toleration of someone outside of the confines of an "educated" person.

There were many times I wanted to speak up in defense of what I knew was true; however, I held my tongue and sought to do the best I could in learning the material.

The semester neared its close with an assigned research paper. The semester grade would rest largely upon that paper. I produced material based upon an element of philosophy that I knew would fit well within the confines of acceptability to the instructor. He was pleased with my work, so much so that when my paper was returned it had received an "A" grade with a comment like: "Excellent work. This shows real intelligence and ability to research and organize."

I now had some evidence I was anxious to use, but still held back, knowing that I had not yet received my final grade for the class.

After finals were over, I awaited my grade report. When it came, I had received an "A." I was a Latter-day Saint, and I had received an "A" in his class. I suspect that was rare, and had he known I was a Mormon, I doubt that I would have been graded so highly.

My day for exposure came. At the end of the following semester I had decided to apply for acceptance for doctoral work. Knowing I needed some references from college professors, I selected the philosophy teacher and made an appointment for a personal interview. When I arrived he was chatting with a graduate student. He invited me in, shook hands, and introduced me to the student. When we were seated in his office, he said "What can I do for you?"

I said: "So that you can recall who I am, here is the research paper I completed in your class last semester with your personal comment on the top; here is my report card with the 'A' I received."

He carefully read both, then looked up. I continued. "I would like to apply for doctoral work at both A.S.U. and B.Y.U. I'd like to know if you would write a recommendation for me."

"You're a Mormon, aren't you!"

"Yes," I replied.

He reread his comment on my research paper. Then he looked up at me and said "It's obvious by my comments that you do intelligent work. How can you justify being a Mormon?"

Having been through his course, I was not about to "rise to the bait" and get hooked. I would not argue with him upon his terms, for I knew I would lose. I simply replied, "I follow a different philosophy than you do."

That seemed to close the door to further pursual, so he made a couple of humorous and off-color jokes about Brigham Young. The other student laughed heartily; I smiled tolerantly. Apparently seeing that he was not getting the usual rise from a Mormon, he turned to the subject I intended to pursue in my doctoral work. We had a rather pleasant conversation about my future studies, and I asked him again if he would write a recommendation for me. He said that he would, and we parted company.

The next few days I was anxious about the prospects of what his recommendation might say. I wondered if I had made a mistake. My fears were dispelled when I received a copy of his letter to my prospective colleges. Of the three professors I had selected for references, the most glowing and complimentary report came from the anti-religious instructor. I noted one comment in his letter to Brigham Young University that carried a connotation they would not recognize: "I suspect that Brent is the type of individual that B.Y.U. might prize most highly." Though couched in complimentary terms, I always wondered whether or not that was intended as a compliment.

I had dispelled in my own mind (and perhaps in his) the concept that Mormons were less intelligent than other students. When understood correctly, Latter-day Saints really ought to be more intelligent than other students. Joseph Smith said, "There is a superior intelligence bestowed upon such as obey the Gospel with full purpose of heart."*

Years later I wrote a poem with my philosophy professor in mind:

"The world is measured by man," he said,
"The senses of man are its gauge.
Emperical evidences, open to all,
Are tools that are used by the sage.

"Consistent experiments isolate truth
And place within anyone's gaze
The gem of existence, the sensibly proofed,
The literal lines of life's maze."

He followed the senses, knew well the books,
Gave many a student his course;
Destroyed with the sword of infallible proof
Any unseen or mystical force.

And so, in his academician way,
Through the halls of high learning he trod,
Gaining knowledge of life in its tangible mode
And missing the knowledge of God.

The brethren of the priesthood were taught that "The most important knowledge in the world is gospel knowledge, and men in the priesthood have available to them the power by which a fulness of gospel knowledge may be had. But that knowledge does not automatically descend upon the head of a man when he is ordained. And the knowledge of the gospel

---

*Joseph Smith, *Teachings of the Prophet Joseph Smith* (Compiled by Joseph Fielding Smith, Salt Lake City, Utah: Deseret Book Company, 1938), p. 67.

contained in the standard works will stay in the standard works unless and until men in the priesthood dig it out for themselves.*

Being a Latter-day Saint does not automatically launch one ahead of nonmembers in intelligence. It does, however, provide a path that will far surpass worldly wisdom when followed.

The question might arise: "Is other learning invaluable if not directly gained from a study of the gospel?"

The answer is no. "To be learned is good *if they hearken unto the counsels of God.*" (2 Nephi 9:29, italics added.) There is a priority for knowledge, however.

"Everyone should learn something new every day. You all have inquiring minds and are seeking truth in many fields. I sincerely hope your greatest search is in the realm of spiritual things, because it is there that we are able to gain salvation and make the progress that leads to eternal life in our Father's kingdom.

"The most important knowledge in the world is gospel knowledge. It is a knowledge of God and his laws, of those things that men must do to work out their salvation with fear and trembling before the Lord. †

All learning does not fit within the category of intelligence. Nephi warned, "O that cunning plan of the evil one! O the vainness, and the frailties, and the foolishness of men! When they are learned they think they are wise, and they hearken not unto the counsel of God, for they set it aside, supposing they know of themselves, wherefore, their wisdom is foolishness and it profiteth them not. And they shall perish." (2 Nephi 9:28.)

Are such individuals learned? Yes. Intelligent? When their wisdom is foolishness and it profiteth them not? And they perish? No. Such are not intelligent.

I used to like to ask my seminary students the following question: "Who is more intelligent—an atheist college professor with five different doctor's degrees in different fields, or a Mormon bishop who only finished high school?"

Invariably the students would select the college professor with five different doctor's degrees as the more intelligent. I would then continue: "Supposing you had to put the future course of the world into the hands of one of those two individuals. Assuming they never changed their lives and philosophies, which would you choose?"

They quickly selected the Mormon bishop.

"Then which of the two is more intelligent?"

The answer seemed obvious, but the students were still a little hesitant.

---

*Priesthood Study Guide, 1974-75, p. 27.
†Joseph Fielding Smith, *Ensign* 1:2, May 1971.

It was difficult for them to discount the five doctoral degrees, but they did so after thinking it through.

Joseph Fielding Smith said: "Intelligence is the light of truth, and we are informed that he who has intelligence or the light of truth will forsake that evil one. A man who has intelligence will worship God and repent of his sins; he will seek to know the will of God and follow it. . . . Now I understand that knowledge is very important, but there is a great fund of knowledge in the possession of men that will not save them in the kingdom of God. What they have got to learn are the fundamental things of the gospel of Jesus Christ. They must learn to obey him. They have got to learn his commandments, his ordinances, and keep them, and unless they do, all their learning and all their knowledge will be of little benefit to them."*

He also said, "The man who is guided by the Holy Spirit and who keeps the commandments of God, who abides in God, will have the clearest understanding and the better judgment always, because he is directed by the Spirit of truth. And the man who relies upon himself, or the knowledge of other men, will not have as clear a vision as will the man who abides in the truth and is directed by the Holy Spirit."†

What is the mark, then, of an intelligent man? It is his closeness to God, as evidenced by his keeping of the commandments and his acquisition of knowledge in a manner that would attest to his faithfulness.

There are many church members who have great knowledge of others' views, but lack in spiritual testimony of that knowledge. To read the words of others is beneficial, but unless the concepts gained are attested to by the spirit of truth, the knowledge is only borrowed, not owned. To read what someone else knows or believes does not constitute personal knowledge. Moroni taught, "And by the power of the Holy Ghost ye may know the truth of all things." (Moroni 10:5.) When the witness of the spirit occurs, the knowledge becomes personal property. One may then attest to the truth from personal knowledge, first hand, and not from borrowed insight.

One of the more impressive witnesses of knowledge that I have heard came from an eight-year-old boy. When he stood at the pulpit he barely reached the microphone. I assumed his testimony would be a nice statement of belief, but instead he said, "I know that the church is true." When he spoke those words, there was a witness from the spirit that reached my heart with power. That boy possessed personal knowledge, and his spiritual I.Q. exceeded many college professors who did not have such a witness and knowledge.

---

*Joseph Fielding Smith, *Doctrines of Salvation, op. cit.,* Vol. 1, pp. 290-291.
†*Doctrines of Salvation,* Vol. 1, p. 229.

What is the beginning outline for the acquisition of intelligence? It is comprised of the first principles and ordinances of the gospel: faith, repentance, baptism, and the reception of the Holy Ghost.

From that point on one may increase in wisdom by seeking knowledge within proper parameters of priority. Whatever field of study or service one enters, a daily and prayerful study of the gospel will be a mark of intelligent direction and an aid to the development of knowledge in any worthy field. Gospel living will insure a continued rate of progress in the acquisition of intelligence.

Soon after I was admitted to a doctoral program at Brigham Young University, my plans for graduate work were interrupted by a call to serve in my ward as bishop. I accepted the calling, thinking that I would have to give up the doctorate in order to serve properly in my priesthood calling. I had not yet begun classes, nor had I designed a study program. To my surprise, prayers led to a feeling that I should not withdraw from the doctoral program, but should pursue it as well as serve as a bishop. (I also had a full-time job.)

My first task in doctoral work was to arrange my priorities, I felt, by putting family and church service first. Before the call to serve as bishop, I had anticipated that it would take me from three to four years to obtain my doctorate. After the call, I assumed five to eight years.

The course toward my degree was difficult, and time never seemed sufficient. But I found that by putting the Lord's work first, I received help with my family, my profession, and my schooling. The doctor's program was completed in a little under two years, and provided one of the more enjoyable growing experiences of my life. I am convinced that if I had put my graduate studies first, pursuing "higher learning" at the expense of church service or family stability, I would have spent more time with less learning and may never have completed the doctoral program.

While the attainment of a doctorate was a thrilling achievement for me, it was not nearly so valuable a learning experience as the day I gained a spiritual witness of the truth of the gospel. On that day, I prayed that I might be sure, as Moroni had promised. The witness I received from the Holy Ghost was unmistakable; it filled me from head to foot with such a wonderful, burning witness that I could never forget the experience, nor would it be dulled with the passing of time. The knowledge of the spirit far surpassed the joy of any other learning achievement, including the reception of a doctor's degree. In fact, I suppose that my testimony experience might be classed as the most "intellectual" experience I have ever had.

When all is said and done, I would suggest that a better measure of intelligence than "I.Q." would be "C.Q."

"They who are of a celestial spirit shall receive the same body which was a natural body . . . and your glory shall be that glory by which your bodies are quickened.

"Ye who are quickened by a portion of the celestial glory shall then receive of the same, even a fulness." (D&C 88:28-29.)

Do you have a "celestial quotient?" Are you of sufficient spirituality and knowledge that you are quickened by a portion of the celestial glory? If so, you are in the upper percentages of intelligent individuals. The spiritual individual is the intelligent one, for the soul that is most like God is the most like the supreme example of intelligence.

> The philosophies
> Of ages
> Will fail
> Miserably
> To match
> The commission:
> "Come, Follow Me."

CHAPTER ELEVEN

Your Conscience: War Or Peace?

Isaiah spoke of a people who were ". . . like the troubled sea, when it cannot rest, whose waters cast up mire and dirt. There is no peace . . ." to such individuals. (Isaiah 57:20-21.) King Benjamin addressed a people who ". . . were filled with joy, having received a remission of their sins, and having peace of conscience . . ." (Mosiah 4:3.)

War or peace? The difference between these two groups can be based upon reaction to conscience.

What is the conscience? It is a special gift given at birth to every human being. It is given by God, and consists of the "spirit" or "light" of Christ. It helps one determine the difference between right and wrong, good and evil. Moroni explained that "The Spirit of Christ is given to every man, that he may know good from evil." (Moroni 7:16.) Of this gift John said, "That was the true Light, which lighteth every man that cometh into the world." (John 1:9.)

When the conscience is heeded, the result is a state of peace, as witnessed by King Benjamin's people. When unheeded, it leads to the state experienced by those spoken of by Isaiah who had no rest. Amulek experienced this conflict when ". . . he began to tremble under a consciousness of his guilt." (Alma 12:1.) John spoke of similar individuals when he said, "And they which heard it, being convicted by their own conscience, went out one by one." (John 8:9.)

The conscience is designed to lead one toward God.

"If a man who has never heard the gospel will hearken to the teachings and manifestations of the Spirit of Christ . . . often spoken of as conscience—

every man has a conscience and knows more or less when he does wrong, and the Spirit guides him if he will hearken to its whisperings—it will lead him eventually to the fulness of the gospel.''*

If not heeded, a state of unrest and conflict will develop that can only be dulled temporarily by resistance. Paul described such individuals when he described them as "Speaking lies in hypocrisy; having their conscience seared with a hot iron." (1 Timothy 4:2.) It may be possible to cauterize the wounded conscience temporarily, but without lasting relief.

If one is enjoying peace of conscience, one is progressing in the right direction. The task is to endure and continue progressing. If one is experiencing war from a troubled conscience, the task is to restore peace. This is done through the process of repentance, so that forgiveness may come. Since every individual (except the Savior) will deal with this process, it would help to take a close look at the pathway for restoration of peace.

Repentance is more than a process to restore personal well being; it is also a commandment to be complied with. When one has sinned, the avoidance of repenting is, in itself, the commission of a serious sin.

"Therefore I command you to repent—repent, lest I smite you by the rod of my mouth, and by my wrath, and by my anger, and your sufferings be sore—how sore you know not, how exquisite you know not, yea, how hard to bear you know not.

"For behold, I God, have suffered these things for all, that they might not suffer if they would repent;

"But if they would not repent they must suffer even as I,

"Which suffering caused myself, even God, the greatest of all, to tremble because of pain, and to bleed at every pore, and to suffer both body and spirit." (D&C 19:15-18.)

"Wherefore, I command you again to repent, lest I humble you with my almighty power; and that you confess your sins, lest you suffer these punishments of which I have spoken." (D&C 19:20.)

What then are the steps of repentance?

First, have a "godly sorrow" for the sins. This is the type of remorse that results in change for the better because of a sorrow produced by knowing that one is not the individual one wants to be. "I am sorry that I did this: I want to change and become better because I know that is the right thing to do." This sorrow is contrasted with the sorrow of the world wherein one is sorry when caught (because of being caught), and not because of a desire to become better. "I am sorry I was stopped and received a fine; it's too bad there was a patrolman nearby."

Paul said, "Now I rejoice, not that ye were made sorry, but that ye sorrowed to repentance: for ye were made sorry after a godly manner, that

---

*Joseph Fielding Smith, *Doctrines of Salvation, op. cit.,* Vol. 1, p. 51.

ye might receive damage by us in nothing. For godly sorrow worketh repentance to salvation not to be repented of: but the sorrow of the world worketh death." (2 Corinthians 7:10.)

Second, build a genuine desire to change your life and make a commitment to clear the problem, no matter what the cost.

When, on occasion, a ward member would approach me as the bishop and confess a serious transgression, I would often ask, "Would you be willing to face a church court if that's what it takes to clear the problem?" Those individuals motivated by a godly sorrow and a resolve to change would always answer "Yes, if that's what it takes." Had one of these individuals hesitated, I would have questioned the sincerity and depth of desire for change. Not all of those individuals were required to face a court, but they had indicated their willingness to repent, whatever the cost.

Third, abandon the sin(s) completely. "And again, believe that ye must repent of your sins and *forsake them.*" (Mosiah 4:10, italics added.) This may mean one will have to abandon unworthy friends, places of temptation, etc. If these sins are not abandoned completely, one brings the weight of former sins back again and finds it increasingly more difficult to change as the sin is repeated.

"And now, verily I say unto you, I, the Lord, will not lay any sin to your charge; go your ways and sin no more; but unto that soul who sinneth shall the former sins return, saith the Lord your God." (D&C 82:7.)

Fourth, make restitution insofar as possible. If one has stolen, the goods must be returned or paid for. If one has misrepresented another, a correction of the information is in order. These types of acts tend to rebuild that which was damaged. As sins become more serious, restitution is more difficult. In sexual sins, restitution is not totally possible. Apologies cannot restore virtue, nor pay for the damage, though immorality can be repented of. In such cases, one must do as much as is practical under the direction of the bishop and the Spirit of the Lord in order to make amends. Then one must live worthily so that the Lord will forgive the difference.

In the case of murder, restitution is not a possibility. Due to the seriousness of this crime, the word of the Lord to the church indicates that "He that kills shall not have forgiveness in this world, nor in the world to come." (D&C 42:18.) It would be to one's advantage, however, to take whatever steps are possible toward repentance, even with unpardonable sins.

Fifth, make confession. All sins need to be confessed to God. The Lord has said, "Behold, he who has repented of his sins, the same is forgiven, and I, the Lord, remember them no more.

"By this ye may know if a man repenteth of his sins—behold, he will confess them and forsake them." (D&C 58:42-43.)

Some sins need to be confessed to the person wronged. This is a part of the restitution process. Stealing, gossip, and cheating would be examples.

Some sins need to be confessed to the bishop or branch president. These include sexual sins, criminal acts such as burglary, theft, etc., apostasy, open opposition to or defiance of the rules and regulations of the church, cruelty to family members, etc.

If confession to the bishop is left out where needed, repentance cannot be completed. A revelation from the Lord says, "Therefore I say unto you, Go; and whosoever transgresseth against me, him shall ye judge according to the sins which he has committed; and if he confess his sins before thee and me, and repenteth in the sincerity of his heart, him shall ye forgive, and I will forgive him also." (Mosiah 26:29.)

Confession is an indication of submission to the requirements of the Lord. It is also a partial payment for sin and a moment for individual judgment. As such, it serves as a powerful object lesson. It is relatively easy to confess a serious wrongdoing in the seclusion of one's own mind; or to pour out a soul in the confidence of one's own room in the still of the night. The hearer is not seen, and not seeing the hearer lightens the embarrassment of failure. But facing someone who knows you, someone whose opinion you value is a different matter. You are looking directly at the bishop. He is looking at you. You are speaking person to person, sight seen.

I think that the Lord is teaching something like this: You have committed a serious transgression. You must realize that you are accountable for your actions in a very real and personal sense. The day will come when you will face me in judgment. No one loves you more than I, so in order to save you the pain and anguish of facing me personally to confess your transgression, I will give you the opportunity to satisfy justice and confess to a representative of mine before the final judgment day arrives. He is your bishop. If you refuse him, you refuse me and must later face me. I want you to feel the emotions of confession in a setting of lesser poignancy than if you were to face me. Then you will understand the reality of judgment so that you may redirect your life in order that our judgmental interview may be pleasant, without remorse. And you will find that your bishop will accept you just as I will when you have met the requirements for forgiveness.

Looking back, there were times when an older member of the ward would make an appointment to share something personal. The individual, who had been living a good life and appeared to be in the prime in gospel satisfaction would break down and cry, confessing a serious transgression that had been committed years before. All of the requirements for forgiveness had been met except one: confession. After wrestling with the conscience unsuccessfully, the repentant member would turn toward the untaken step. When the confession was completed, a tremendous burden was lifted and a peace of mind settled in its place. Joy replaced anxiety and peace superseded the war with conscience.

When confession is required, it is a serious mistake to postpone it.

There are special circumstances where confession is needed before the congregation of the church. These sins are ones that have become public knowledge and that need a public clearing of the record. One should only take this step as guided by the bishop and the Spirit of the Lord. It is generally not good to make public one's sins and faults.

A confession is best initiated by the transgressor. A forced confession is not indicative of sincere repentance.

In order to clear one's slate, a complete confession is required. Details of the sins may not be appropriate, but the confession of one serious sin at the exclusion of another is not sufficient. If there is any doubt, it would pay to sweep the corners of the mind so that one need not leave the bishop's office wondering if something else should have been confessed. Nothing unclean should be left behind to fester.

Sixth, live all of the commandments of the Lord. One cannot be forgiven for transgression of one of the commandments while knowingly violating another. "For whosoever shall keep the whole law, and yet offend in one point, he is guilty of all." (James 2:10.)

"And again, every person who belongeth to this church of Christ, shall observe to keep all the commandments and covenants of the church." (D&C 42:78.)

One cannot request forgiveness for cheating while refusing to give up the sin of lying. One cannot say, "I will stop smoking in order to be forgiven, but I intend to keep drinking coffee."

Seventh, forgive others. This implies the application of the golden rule. If you would be forgiven, forgive others. In the parable of the debt and the harsh servant, the forgiven one refused to extend the same compassion. "Then his lord, after that he had called him, said unto him, O thou wicked servant, I forgave thee all that debt, because thou desiredst me:

"Shouldest not thou also have had compassion on thy fellowservant, even as I had pity on thee?

"And his lord was wroth, and delivered him to the tormentors, till he should pay all that was due unto him.

"So likewise shall my heavenly Father do also unto you, if ye from your hearts forgive not every one his brother their traspasses." (Matthew 18:32-35.)

In the language of modern scripture, "I, the Lord, will forgive whom I will forgive, but of you it is required to forgive all men." (D&C 64:10.)

Eighth, possible withdrawal of fellowship or church membership as a step in repentance. This means disfellowshipment or excommunication for those sins set forth by the Lord as being serious enough to merit court action. The bishop or stake president is the key judge to make such determinations under the direction of the spirit.

Having sat in on several church courts, I found them to be courts of love rather than courts of retribution. The transgressor, having made known the nature of his sins and his desire for repentance, would then have the opportunity to have some of the best of the Lord's servants prayerfully consider his case and the course that would most likely help him back into the grace of the Lord in the shortest amount of time—not that time and brevity were considerations, but that the transgressor need not be channeled down a less effective path for recovery than might be available. When, after discussion and prayers a court decision was reached, it was done with the inspiration of the Lord taking precedence over the reasoning of men, and was made for the good of the individual.

A person deserving disfellowshipment or excommunication, as difficult as those roads will be, will lose a great blessing and lengthen his time of suffering by seeking to cover up a sin that requires court action.

The length of time for disfellowshipment or excommunication is determined by the quality of one's repentance as well as the seriousness of the transgression. No rule of time has been set, but it is likely that the penalty will be effected for sufficient time to insure a complete payment for sin and a proof of total commitment and desire to return to the fold. This amount of time is generally not short.

What happens if a person deserving a church court fails to repent and is not brought to justice? The answer is given in the scriptures.

"Behold, verily I say unto you, there are hypocrites among you, who have deceived some, which has given the adversary power; but behold such shall be reclaimed; [the deceived ones]

"But the hypocrites shall be detected and shall be cut off, either in life or in death, even as I will; and wo unto them who are cut off from my church, for the same are overcome of the world." (D&C 50:7-8.)

Those who miss the action of a church court in this life will find it waiting in the next. It would be much better to face the court in mortality than to deal with the problems in the spirit world, for one can repent easier in mortality with the spirit and body together than in the spirit world while the body lies in the grave.

Delbert L. Stapley gave this insight: "We must recognize that mortality has been granted to us as a probationary state where all physical appetites are to be mastered. It is far more difficult to repent in the spirit world of sins which involve physical habits and actions.

"It is obvious we either discipline our lives here, or pay the price for the undisciplined life in the world to come.*

The prophet Alma expressed it in this way:

---

*The Ensign, Nov. 1977, p. 20.

"For behold, this life is the time for men to prepare to meet God; yea, behold the day of this life is the day for men to perform their labors.

"And now, as I said unto you before, as ye have had so many witnesses, therefore, I beseech of you that ye do not procrastinate the day of your repentance until the end; for after this day of life, which is given us to prepare for eternity, behold, if we do not improve our time while in this life, then cometh the night of darkness wherein there can be no labor performed.

"Ye cannot say, when ye are brought to that awful crises, that I will repent, that I will return to my God. Nay, ye cannot say this; for that same spirit which doth possess your bodies at the time that ye go out of this life, that same spirit will have power to possess your body in that eternal world." (Alma 34:32-34.)

It is obvious that the time guideline for repentance is "the sooner, the better." Procrastination merely adds to one's sins and burden of guilt and makes the repentance process longer and more difficult.

Is there an order to the steps of repentance? Not for all people at all times. All necessary steps must be completed, but the order may vary. One individual may confess to the bishop and then make restitution; another might make restitution and then confess. Still another may not need to confess to the bishop because the sin was minor and correctable without taking that step.

Recognition of sin and a sorrow for the transgression must hold early places in the order of repentance, with other steps following. Completeness, however, is more important than order.

The whole process of repentance has been revealed as an aid to personal growth and a means of achieving peace and joy. There are two types of forgiveness that may be granted: one from the bishop (or presiding ecclesiastical authority) and one from the Lord.

Forgiveness by the bishop means that one will not be brought before a church court for trial concerning church membership. It means that no penalty will be imposed. It does not necessarily mean that the Lord has forgiven the transgression. The transgressor must still continue the process of repentance until the Lord clears the slate. When this occurs, one's conscience is cleared of guilt by a peaceful witness from the Lord that one's sins will not be remembered or brought up any more, including on the day of judgment. One is no longer held "guilty" for those transgressions. As President Spencer W. Kimball said, "The essence of the miracle of forgiveness is that it brings peace to the previously anxious, restless, frustrated, perhaps tormented soul."*

King Benjamin's people sensed this inner peace. "And it came to pass that after they had spoken these words the Spirit of the Lord came upon

---

*Spencer W. Kimball, *The Miracle of Forgiveness, op. cit.,* p. 363.

them, and they were filled with joy, having received a remission of their sins, and having *peace of conscience,* because of the exceeding faith which they had in Jesus Christ.'' (Mosiah 4:3, italics added.)

So might each individual find peace of conscience. When internal war is caused by transgression, the plan of repentance is available for a restitution of peace and joy.

The best course for humanity to follow, of course, is to be perfect. The Lord has so commanded. Since the Savior was the only perfect example, our goal is to stray as little as possible and repent as quickly as possible whenever we falter. By so doing, peace will be our lot rather than war.

As to the ultimate decision to ''Your conscience: war or peace?''—it is up to you.

CHAPTER TWELVE

Behold, Are Ye Stripped Of Pride?

"Be thou humble; and the Lord thy God shall lead thee by the hand, and give thee answer to thy prayers." (D&C 112:10.) How often I have pondered the security and love of such a condition. To walk hand in hand with the Lord, completely trusting in His will and direction, as a young child does his father, is a beautiful concept. Humility seems to be a major key, and to attain humility one must be stripped of pride—the kind of pride that leads to self-centeredness and self-dependency at the cost of spiritual direction.

One of the fond pictures retained in my mind is that of walking hand in hand with a little daughter of about three or four years of age. How completely she trusted me, and how I loved guiding her by the hand. There was a bond of love and respect between us. My hand extended down, and hers reached up.

Perhaps that is symbolic of the relationship we have with the Lord: He reaches down, and we reach up. The Lord said, "For my thoughts are not your thoughts, neither are your ways my ways . . .

"For as the heavens are higher than the earth, so are my ways higher than your ways, and my thoughts than your thoughts." (Isaiah 55:8-9.)

Perhaps it is when we fail to reach up that we lose the grip and begin to fall toward the clutches of pride.

I've had the experience of trying things on my own, without reaching up to the Lord. Even when done unintentionally, the failure and loss of self-esteem has been difficult to bear. Then there were the times when I felt totally unqualified to answer a need, such as a request for a special blessing.

Reaching up in prayer, I petitioned the Lord for His direction and guidance that another servant might be blessed, and found the heavens opened to my mind to satisfy the need.

On one such occasion, I was setting apart an elders quorum presidency during a priesthood meeting. Each blessing flowed with an individual uniqueness for each brother. After the meeting, a priesthood holder came to me and said in a complimentary way, "You have a golden tongue." I smiled, knowing that both he and I knew the source of the blessings, and I mentally passed the compliment on to He who really deserved it.

I have found that the great men I have known are all humble men, inspired of the Lord. They never consider themselves as great, but rather as servants of the Lord and their fellowmen. I used to be afraid of great men, such as leaders in the church. Then I had the opportunity to serve with some of them on local levels and meet some of them on higher levels. I lost the fear, and replaced it with love and respect. They were humble men, and that's what made them great in my eyes.

I recall having received my first call to serve in a bishopric in a university ward in Tempe, Arizona. I went to my first stake meeting for bishoprics. The stake president (president George Dana) was a well-known and highly respected man, the kind of individual whose shadow I would hardly have dared to pass through. I entered the high council room alone, prior to the beginning of the meeting. Many of the seats were occupied, and President Dana was busily engaged in transacting some business with another church leader. When he looked around and saw me entering, he immediately stopped his conversation, rose to his feet, walked over to me, and warmly shook my hand. He probably never thought twice about the action, but for such a great individual to rise at my coming, I felt as honored as if a king had greeted me. I was so impressed that I recorded the experience in my personal journal as one of the rich experiences of my life, representative of the greatness of the president and the honor I felt that he would extend such a courtesy to me. I was the newest and hence the least of the brethren, he was the longest in service and the greater in authority. Yet he rose to greet me. And I learned a lesson in humility.

The disciples once approached Jesus and asked, "Who is the greatest in the kingdom of heaven?

"And Jesus called a little child unto him, and set him in the midst of them,

"And said, Verily I say unto you, Except ye be converted, and become as little children, ye shall not enter into the kingdom of heaven.

"Whosoever therefore shall humble himself as this little child, the same is greatest in the kingdom of heaven." (Matthew 18:1-4.)

What does it mean to humble oneself as a little child? King Benjamin gave insight as he addressed his people and taught:

"For the natural man is an enemy to God, and has been from the fall of Adam, and will be, forever and ever, unless he yields to the enticings of the Holy Spirit, and putteth off the natural man and becometh a saint through the atonement of Christ the Lord, *and becometh as a child, submissive, meek, humble, patient, full of love, willing to submit to all things which the Lord seeth fit to inflict upon him, even as a child doth submit to his father.*" (Mosiah 3:19, italics added.)

To leave the following of instinct and the drive for self-preservation (as found in the animals of nature) and to follow the promptings of the Spirit, becoming as a child in the virtues of a divine parent-child relationship, is to become great in the kingdom. Such greatness is not highlighted by a spotlight and applause on the stage of humanity, but by the quiet love that flows from divine approval.

The greatness of humility is also evident outside of church circles. However, it is also typical in the business world to find executives who think they are great and act as if they are great. In salary and authority over others, they may be great. But as human beings, they are often left wanting in the balance, lacking the quality of true greatness: humility.

One of the nonmembers of the church who became an influence upon my life was the president of a large steel company. It was a stroke of good fortune that allowed me to meet him.

That fortune began one day when my father came home from his day of work at the steel plant and asked if I would compose a song for him. There was a contest for the workers to come up with safety slogans and motivational sayings, and he thought a song would be unique. I responded by composing a tune with lyrics which my friend (Neal Adams) and I tape recorded. Dad took it to the steel plant and it was so well received that they bought the copyright and paid to have it professionally recorded. We were invited to meet the president of the steel company and have our pictures taken with him. In meeting the president, I was immediately impressed with his graciousness and humility. We were the honored ones, yet he made us feel as if it was his pleasure to be with us. He was the president, we were the workers; yet he made us feel as if we honored him by being there.

I learned that the steel workers highly respected this president. I was told that sometimes at night a custodian would enter the president's office with cleaning materials only to discover that the president was working late at his desk. As the custodian would turn to leave, the president would invite him to come in and continue his work. He would move out of the way so that cleaning could be done, visit with the worker, ask his opinion and feelings about the plant, etc.

The last time I visited with this great man was in a reception line honoring him as he was about to leave the state to begin a new assignment back East. I was determined to compliment him and get the last word in, for he had a way of turning a compliment around so that the complimentor felt complimented. I told him how I felt about him, and sure enough, he turned it around so that I felt complimented even more. I tried again, and he succeeded again. A third time I made the effort, and a third time he elevated me a little more than I had elevated him. I gave up, and continued on through the line with a respect for a man whose greatness was in his ability to make others feel great.

Sometimes it is difficult to notice when pride slips in and weakens humility. I had struggled with pride in my growing-up years, failed several times, and learned some hard lessons. My successes came when I reached up to the Lord for divine help and then recognized the source of my strength. But sometimes, pride had a way of leaving a residue that I overlooked.

When I was assigned to the Institute program in Church Education, I moved from Utah to Clifornia. I had just completed service as a bishop and had also graduated from B.Y.U. with a doctorate in education. My wife and I had sung together in the Mormon Tabernacle Choir. I had gained some respect as a speaker prior to our move. As we left for California, I thought, "Now I can really make a contribution to the Institute program. I have a background that is special, and I have something to offer."

The first year was difficult. People did not flock to hear me speak or teach as I had anticipated. The doctor's degree seemed to make little difference in building the program. Singing with the Tabernacle Choir was a nicety that helped little in succeeding with my work. Discouragement came, and I wondered what I had to offer. Everything I thought I had to contribute seemed to make little difference, and I told myself that anyone could do as well as I was doing without my credentials.

Then I received an opportunity to speak in an education-week circuit. Now, I thought, I could make a unique contribution. As the congregations had been filled with appreciative people when I had spoken in meetings in Utah, I anticipated having full rooms during my lectures. Again I was disappointed. My room was occasionally well-filled, but often only partially occupied by listeners. The crowd seemed to flock to the chapel, and I failed to draw a full house.

That seemed to be the final straw. The one thing I thought I had left didn't pull through as I had hoped. While my listeners were very responsive, I judged success by the ability to fill the room with people, and I hadn't attained that measure.

As I was driving home from lecturing in a distant city, I was very despondent. "Why did I come to California? I haven't made any difference at all. I'm not contributing anything that anyone else couldn't do." While deep in thoughts of failure, the voice of the Lord came into my mind and said, "Behold, are ye stripped of pride?"

I was startled. I recognized the words as a quote from Book of Mormon scriptures (Alma 5:28), although I didn't know where it was found at the time. I pondered the saying, for I had not really felt a sense of unrighteous pride as I anticipated my abilities and efforts at building the program. Yet that voice was clear, and I responded, "Yes, I am now."

It seemed as if every talent I possessed had been stripped from me like old wallpaper from a wall. The final peeling was of speaking ability sufficient to draw a crowd. I thought that was my final chance to be a real influence, and I didn't do what I thought I could do. There was nothing left. I sat alone, stripped of pride. The lesson was hard, but necessary and beneficial.

The success did begin to come later on. But when it did, the residue of pride had been cleaned up, replaced by a respect for divine help and a Father in Heaven who merited the compliments of success. I depended more upon Him than my talents and abilities.

Now I try my best to be humble and avoid the subtle, self-righteous pride that blocks success. I suspect, however, that if I had a lesson to give on humility, the Lord would again point out a few things to me that I had missed. I even hesitate to try to define humility, lest I miss the mark myself.

As a young high priest, I marveled at the wisdom and strength of my bishop, Jay Turley. Serving as one of his counselors, I viewed his position with awe and respect. He seemed to be the ultimate source of strength and wisdom. Then one day he called me into his office and explained that he was going to be out of the country during most of the coming summer. He explained that I, as his first counselor, would assume the role of acting bishop. I was astounded at the idea, as well as overwhelmed. Expecting a long lecture or training session, I asked, "What will I do?" His total inservice training session lasted about three seconds as he said, "Oh, you'll know what to do." That was basically all he told me.

The summer came and my role began. In prayer I had approached the Lord and asked for help. The ward members began coming to me for advice, blessings, and help in solving complex problems. I learned quickly what the bishop meant when he said, "Oh, you'll know what to do." There was an increase of wisdom and intelligence that flowed to me as the acting bishop— something greater than I had before the bishop left. It was a gift from the Lord in behalf of His saints. Problems became easier to solve and there was a Spirit that guided me consistently in the right direction. The experience was wonderful.

The summer drew to a close. I did not know the exact day that the bishop was to return; neither did he. I was walking through our home one afternoon when I literally felt something leave me. I called out to my wife, "Janene: Bishop Turley is back." She asked how I knew, and I just said, "I know." I finished the work I was engaged in, then called the bishop's home about an hour later. He answered his phone and expressed surprise that I had called when he had only arrived about an hour earlier. I told him I had a feeling that he had returned. The mantle had left me, and whatever it was, its absence was apparent.

The bishop assumed his regular role, and I found that complex problems were not so easily solved: it often took the bishop to reach the correct solutions. I told my councilor friend that I felt less intelligent now that I was no longer the acting bishop. The mantle of authority had moved to another.

When I was called to be a bishop years later, I knew where the strength of the calling would lie. With my ordination at the hands of Elder Sterling W. Sill, the mantle of authority rested upon me again and I knew the source of my strength and intelligence.

When my service closed with a release, I anticipated the letdown that would come with the loss of that mantle. Knowing the source and purpose of that extra help and authority, it was easier for me to make the adjustment and assume another role in the church. The strength was correctly attributed to the Lord, but He was to be gracious and teach me an interesting lesson I had not anticipated.

After my release, I was flying down to southern California to be oriented to my new church education assignment. I sat on the plane next to an older woman. Neither of us had spoken to the other as yet, and I was reviewing in my mind how I might approach her and perhaps do a little missionary work. While I was trying to think of a friendly approach to this woman whom I had never seen before, she turned to me and said, "You're a bishop, aren't you!"

Startled, I replied, "Why, yes . . . I used to be."

She said nothing more, so I smiled at her and said "The suit and tie gave me away, huh?"

"Nope."

"What made you think I was a bishop?"

"When I saw you, I just had a feeling you were a bishop."

The stewardess then advised her that she could have another seat nearer the front of the plane and the sister left. I didn't have a chance to visit with her again. As I reviewed the exchange, I felt the thought come to me, "Once a bishop, always a bishop. I guess I shouldn't have said *used to be*. The Lord is teaching me a lesson. I am still a bishop."

I felt that the mantle had not entirely left, but that there was a portion remaining as a blessing for service rendered.

I've come to feel that the greatest men in the church are the most humble men, who know that the source of their strength lies in the Lord whom they serve. I think the humblest authority of them all is the Lord Himself.

In 1977, my wife and I participated in a tour of the Holy Land. Our church education group was seated near Bethlehem, referred to as "Mormons' Shepherds' Field." We read some passages of scripture relating the story of the birth of Jesus. We sang some Christmas carols, changing the title of "Far, Far Away on Judea's Plain" to "Near, Near at Hand . . ."

I wondered what it must have been like for the shepherds to gaze up into the heavens and hear the angelic host announcing the birth of the Savior of the world, heralding the event with divine song. I gazed across the rolling hills of Bethlehem, contemplating the sacred event.

Our tour director broke my chain of thought with the announcement that it was time to start back toward the bus. The others began to stroll back, but I remained to change the film in my camera. After doing so, I decided to walk around a little knoll to my left to see if there was anything different. As I rounded the knoll, I walked face to face with a donkey that had been quietly grazing, unseen by any of the tourists. As I gazed into the eyes of the donkey, time seemed to pause while the Lord took advantage of a teaching moment. I was impressed with the aura of total humility in the face of the strong but silent animal. I thought of this animal's mission in life: to bear the burdens placed upon him by mankind. Then I thought of the Savior's triumphal entry into Jerusalem. Approaching the supreme act of His life's mission, he rode, not on a great stallion, but on a humble little donkey. And as the donkey's role was to bear the burdens of mankind, so would the Savior bear the burdens of His brothers and sisters of the world during the atoning sacrifice. His greatness was enhanced by His humility. The object lesson of the donkey on the hills near Bethlehem gave me a deeper feeling of respect and love for my Savior. Like other saints, I stood all amazed at the love Jesus offered me.

Sometimes, now, when things seem to be going well for me in life, I pause for a safety check, and ask myself the question: "Behold, are ye stripped of pride?"

CHAPTER THIRTEEN

Eternal Roots

There has been a surge in the genealogical task of tracing one's "roots." The mortal limit in the line of progenitors would be Adam and Eve. With latter-day revelation, the limits may be extended even further back, to eternal roots.

In the ninety-third section of the Doctrine and Covenants we are told, "Man was also in the beginning with God. Intelligence, or the light of truth, was not created or made, neither indeed can be." (D&C 93:29.) I never felt comfortable with the idea that I always existed. If I never had a beginning, how could I be a child of God? If I existed forever, how could He be my father?

Marion G. Romney said, "In origin, man is a son of God. The spirits of men 'are begotten sons and daughters unto God' (D&C 76:24). Through that birth process, self-existing intelligence was organized into individual spirit beings.*

Brother Bruce R. McConkie taught that "All men were first born in pre-existence as the literal *spirit offspring* of God our Heavenly Father. This birth constituted the beginning of the human ego as a conscious identity. By the ordained procreative process our exalted and immortal Father begat his spirit progeny in pre-existence."†

As individuals, we all had beginnings; that occurred when each of us was born as a spirit child to a Heavenly Father and Mother. The material of

---

The Ensign, Nov. 1978, p. 14.

†Bruce R. McConkie, *Mormon Doctrine* (Salt Lake City, Utah: Bookcraft Publishers, 1966, p. 84. See also, *Teachings of the Prophet Joseph Smith, op. cit.,* footnote 5, p. 158.

which we were composed was an eternal substance, having no beginning nor end. Our bodies were made of eternal matter, formed and delivered through the birth process.

With this birth and beginning in the pre-existence, every child received a beautiful inheritance. We are taught that in order to obtain the highest degree in the celestial kingdom, we must be united properly in marriage. (D&C 131:1-4.) Among the blessings of the attainment of that highest kingdom are exaltation and a continuation of the seeds forever. (D&C 132:19.) This means that only perfect individuals, exalted in the highest degree of celestial life, may have spirit children. That in turn means that every spirit child was born to a perfect set of parents. There were no tendencies toward weakness or imperfection that were inherited. Everyone had an equal beginning in that sense. No failures could be blamed on society or parents. Each child was born innocent, with a heritage from celestial beings who were perfect.

After our pre-mortal births, what did we do? "We lived in this premortal life with him [Father in Heaven] for an infinite period of time. We were on probation; we were being schooled and tested and examined; we were given the laws and the circumstances so that we could progress and advance . . .

"In this prior life, this premortal existence, this preexistence, we developed various capacities and talents. Some developed them in one field and some in another. The most important of all fields was the field of spirituality, the ability, the talent, the capacity to recognize truth."*

Joseph Fielding Smith explained, "God gave his children their agency even in the spirit world, by which the individual spirits had the privilege, just as men have here, of choosing the good and rejecting the evil, or partaking of the evil to suffer the consequences of their sins . . . some even there were more faithful than others in keeping the commandments of the Lord. . . .

"The spirits of men . . . had an equal start, and we know they were all innocent in the beginning; but the right of free agency which was given to them enabled some to out-strip others, and thus, through the eons of immortal existence, to become more intelligent, more faithful, for they were free to act for themselves, to think for themselves, to receive the truth or rebel against it."†

After our spirits were born, we were given the opportunity to learn and progress toward a state that Heavenly Father enjoyed. There were commandments to follow and choices to make; from that point on we became

*For further information, see 1975-76 Priesthood Study Guide, *When Thou Art Converted, Strengthen Thy Brethren*, pp. 8-9.
†Joseph Fielding Smith, *Doctrines of Salvation, op. cit.*, Vol. 1, pp. 58-59.

unequal because of variance in use of free agency. While some excelled, others did not. The use of free agency led to conflict, culminating in what is referred to as "the war in heaven."

At some point in pre-mortal existence, a climax was reached in which a crossroad appeared and many turned away from the pathway of progress. At a grand council, Jesus sustained Heavenly Father's true plan leading to happiness and eternal life; Satan, a liar from the beginning, presented a false plan guaranteeing success, but which was inherently unable to produce the results. Following the presentations and the decision by most to follow the correct plan, ". . . there was war in heaven: Michael [Adam—see D&C 27:11] and his angels fought against the dragon; and the dragon fought and his angels,

"And prevailed not; neither was their place found any more in heaven.

"And the great dragon was cast out, that old serpent, called the Devil, and Satan, which deceiveth the whole world: he was cast out into the earth, and his angels were cast out with him." (Revelation 12:7-9.)

This conflict was settled and won by those who accepted the atonement and had the power of testimony (see Revelation 12:11).

Thus a third part of those spirit beings failed the test of the first estate (see Abraham 3:26, Revelation 12:4).

Among those who passed the test of the first estate, plans were effected for the accomplishment of the tests of the second estate, life upon this earth. The most faithful were assigned to enter mortality through a chosen lineage. This lineage was made up of those people now referred to as Israelites."

"Israel is an eternal people. Members of that chosen race first gained their inheritance with the faithful in the pre-mortal life. Israel was a distinct people in the preexistence. Many of the valiant and noble spirits in that first estate were chosen, elected, and foreordained to be born into the family of Jacob, so as to be natural heirs of all the blessings of the gospel."*

Based upon special worthiness, many spirits were elected (chosen and selected) to be born into the second estate of existence (mortality) through the lineage of a covenant people, referred to as the Lord's people, or Israelites.

While this blessing guaranteed a birth into mortality through a certain lineage, it did not guarantee successful completion of mortality, for that again, as in the pre-mortal existence, would depend upon the use of free agency. Neither did it exclude any not born in that lineage from accepting the truth and being "adopted" into the group referred to as the Lord's people.

---

*Bruce R. McConkie, *Doctrinal New Testament Commentary,* (Salt Lake City, Utah: Bookcraft, Inc., 1973), Vol. 2, p. 284.

In the pre-mortal existence, a special patriarchal-type blessing was given to many of these spirit individuals. This blessing was referred to as a "foreordination."

"Now the Lord had shown unto me, Abraham, the intelligences that were organized [through the birth process] before the world was; and among all these there were many of the noble and great ones; And God saw these souls that they were good, and he stood in the midst of them, and he said: These I will make my rulers; for he stood among those that were spirits, and he saw that they were good; and he said unto me: Abraham, thou art one of them; thou wast chosen before thou wast born." (Abraham 3:23.)

These pre-mortal blessings for future accomplishment were based, as all blessings, upon continued worthiness.

Having had these types of opportunities, experiences, and blessings, we entered into the mortal phase of existence. Through the birth process, a mortal body was organized to house our spirits. All were again born innocent, but not equal. Preexistent qualities were brought with the spirit.*

The mortal phase of existence becomes the most important phase. In the words of Joseph Fielding Smith, "This life is the most vital period in our eternal existence."†

In the words of Alma, "For behold, this life is the time for men to prepare to meet God." (Alma 34:32.)

Because many do not prove faithful in the mortal phase of existence, the blessings of election will be lost.

"The house of Israel was a distinct people in preexistence; that is, by obedience and devotion, certain of the spirit children of the Father earned the right to be born in the lineage of Abraham, of Isaac, and of Jacob, and of being natural heirs to the blessings of the gospel. But some of them, after such a favored birth, after being numbered with the chosen seed, turn from the course of righteousness and become children of the flesh; that is, they walk after the manner of the world, rejecting the spiritual blessings held in store for Israel. They are disinherited; they shall not continue as children in the family of the prophets when the chosen race continues as a distinct people in the eternal worlds. Thus they are descendants of the prophets in this life but shall not inherit with the sons of God in the life to come."‡

President Lee explained that ". . . there are many who were foreordained before the world was, to a greater state than they have prepared themselves for here. Even though they might have been among the noble and great, from among whom the Father declared he would make his chosen leaders, they may fail of that calling here in mortality."§

---

*For more information, see *Conference Report,* April 1974, pp. 101-103.

†Joseph Fielding Smith, *Doctrines of Salvation, op. cit.,* Vol. 1, p. 69.

‡Bruce R. McConkie, *Doctrinal New Testament Commentary, op. cit.,* Vol. 2, pp. 276-277.

§For further information, see *Conference Report,* Oct. 1973, p. 7.

Hence, the roots established in pre-mortality may be dislodged in mortality, if not nourished by obedience to the gospel plan.

Members of the church have already been called to the gospel. It is likely that they received an election in the pre-mortal state to be born in a chosen lineage to the earth. What would it mean to have a calling and election made sure? It would mean that sufficient proof has been given that one qualifies to have that calling and election sealed forever, never to be lost. Then one enters the state referred to by the Apostle Paul:

"The Spirit itself beareth witness with our spirit, that we are the children of God:

"And if children, then heirs; heirs of God, and joint heirs with Christ." (Romans 8:16-17.)

Peter challenged the saints to ". . . give diligence to make your calling and election sure: for if ye do these things, ye shall never fall:

"For so an entrance shall be ministered unto you abundantly into the everlasting kingdom of our Lord and Saviour Jesus Christ." (2 Peter 1:10-11.)

With a knowledge of eternal roots, may we all strive to keep those roots firmly established in the soil of the gospel that the fruits of eternal life may be enjoyed in the next phase of existence where mortality will be viewed as genealogy of the past.

CHAPTER FOURTEEN

Insights Through Music

The Savior's love for little children is exemplified in the Book of Mormon when, during his visit to the righteous Nephites and Lamanites, he blessed the children one by one, wept for joy, and said:

"Behold, your little ones.

"And as they looked to behold they cast their eyes towards heaven, and they saw the heavens open, and they saw angels descending out of heaven as it were in the midst of fire; and they came down and encircled those little ones about, and they were encircled about with fire; and the angels did minister unto them." (3 Nephi 17:23-24.)

His love for music is evident in the declaration "For my soul delighteth in the song of the heart; yea, the song of the righteous is a prayer unto me, and it shall be answered with a blessing upon their heads." (D&C 25:12.)

Can you imagine the expression one might see on the Savior's face as He stands by a primary or junior Sunday School class, listening to them sing "I Am A Child Of God?" Perhaps, if you could correctly imagine that expression, you would weep for joy as He did at the marvelous scene recorded in third Nephi.

It is natural and beautiful for young children to sing, and in so doing they are learning to pray. Prayers carried on the wings of song bring blessings. It is not necessary to be accomplished to be acceptable, for the Lord declared it was the "song of the righteous" He accepted. There was no implication as to musical ability above others. So children singing are children praying, and the Savior's heart is touched by such beauty.

The Savior said "Except ye be converted, and become as little children, ye shall not enter into the kingdom of heaven." (Matthew 18:3.) When adults and youth sing with the feeling and openness of children, they too bring blessings upon themselves and joy to their Lord. We should sing, just as we should pray.

My earliest remembrances of song come from my primary and junior Sunday School days. The messages of the gospel were joined in the sweetness of song, and the impression of such music has had a lasting and strengthening effect upon my life.

There are many benefits that come from music. It was not until my participation in the a cappella choir in high school that I began to realize more fully some of those benefits.

Each day as I sang with the choir, my spirits were lifted. I felt better, happier, more enthusiastic for life. When we sang of deity, I sensed a feeling of awe and respect for the Lord. When we sang of our country, a feeling of pride and patriotism welled up inside. Whatever the song, I found that I could feel more deeply the emotions of the music and lyrics. Emotional stability increased, and my ability to worship carried over into the songs within our church services.

I particularly remember the thrill of singing Handel's "Messiah" for the first time. All of the music groups within our high school joined for a grand performance at Christmas time. The choirs were on the risers, the band and orchestra on the stage above. The auditorium seats were filled up and into the balcony, with people standing along the walls for the performance.

I had been told that during the singing of the "Hallelujah Chorus" the audience would rise to its feet in respect. I was ready mentally, but not emotionally. When we began to sing the first "hallelujah" the rush of sound as people rose to their feet brought an overwhelming sense of respect for the Lord. I was touched to the point of tears, as were many other singers and the director, Brother Richard Dastrup. What started as a song ended as a declaration of worship from the heart. Feeling and song combined in adoration of the Christ.

I have often wondered about the composition of the Messiah by Handel. Was he composing or remembering?

I believe pre-mortal talent and appreciation for music carries over into mortality. Handel composed that monumental work in such a short time that I believe pre-mortal preparation, as well as direct inspiration from the Lord, flowed through the talent of Handel.

In the a cappella choir at Brigham Young University I found that the same feelings I had for music in high school were continued and deepened. Spirits were again lifted, the messages of the lyrics felt more deeply, and the ability to worship increased.

An opportunity to testify of the truthfulness of the gospel through the medium of song came with an invitation to sing at the Music Educators'

National Convention in St. Louis, Missouri. Out choir, under the direction of Dr. Ralph Woodward, was honored to be invited. We were doubly honored in that we were told that our trip would be a missionary and pioneering effort. We were to sing to a gentile audience the message of the gospel. The impression that many educators had of our choir would likely be the impression they would carry of the church. We were both honored and frightened to represent not only the university's music department, but also the church to which we belonged.

On the day our choir was scheduled to sing at the convention, we gathered (prior to performance) in a room to offer our silent individual prayers. A choir spokesman petitioned the Lord and requested that we might have the privilege and ability to sing with the heart as well as the voice, that our song might be a testimony of the gospel to a nonmember audience. We prayed that we might do well musically, for we had heard comments indicating that many did not feel that much would come from our group, for we were "Mormons." They did not feel that a Mormon group could measure up to the high standards of music performance to which they were accustomed.

As we filed out of the room toward the stage, we passed the orchestra members who were taking a break. Many were smoking cigarettes and visiting noisely. When we came into their view, they turned to watch and became silent. We felt the eyes of the gentiles were already upon us, and we sensed keenly the need for the Lord's spirit. As we entered on stage, the huge audience quieted to a hush even before we were announced. Each choir member's heart was lifted in a prayer for success.

We began singing a work titled "The Articles Of Faith" by Merrill Bradshaw. We were presenting the teachings and beliefs of our church through song.

We sang of the Godhead, the atonement, the creation and fall, the principles and ordinances of the gospel. We were singing our belief in scriptures, of the Bible as far as it was translated correctly, and were about to sing of the Book of Mormon when something unexpected occurred.

When we had finished the words "as far as it is translated correctly," a spirit enveloped the entire choir and figuratively lifted us from the stage. Elevated by the Spirit of the Lord, we sang . . . no, we *testified* that "we also believe the Book of Mormon to be the word of God." Eyes were moist, and hearts were full with the testimony of truth clothed in the beauty of song.

The last article of faith declared the virtues for which we, as a people, sought. The monumental work ended with the sisters singing in simple, quiet beauty, ". . . if there is anything virtuous, lovely, or of good report or praiseworthy, we seek after these things." (Article of Faith 13.) The last note was held softly, then cut off delicately. There was a moment of silence in the auditorium. How had we done? Had the message gotten through? Did we represent the church well? Would the audience be tolerantly polite in their applause, or enthusiastic in response to musical accomplishment? It was but a second or two when the applause broke like a clap of thunder. Jumping to their feet, the music educators applauded and shouted for what seemed like an eternity. We had done well; our prayers had been heard and answered, and our hearts touched. We had testified for the Lord by the power of His strength, and we felt it. The audience had seen something of worth coming from "the Mormons."

On the way home from our performance, we had another touching moment. We stood as a choir around the preserved remains of the Liberty Jail where Joseph had lain, falsely imprisoned. Brother Woodward stood on the floor of the jail and directed us in song. With the vicarious memory of Joseph lying perhaps where Brother Woodward stood, we sang again from the heart, "we have endured many things." Then with a courage for the future born from the hope of the past, we testified in song "and hope to be able to endure all things." Tears sealed the testimony of college students uniting their voices in the prayer of song.

Later I participated with the choir in making a record. One of the songs we recorded told of the trek of the pioneers. As I sang that work, I developed a keen sense of appreciation and feeling for our pioneer heritage. I could almost see the men, women and children trudging across the plains, the cold and bitter nights, the shoveling in of shallow graves upon pioneers of all ages. There was something about music that both heightened and deepened the message of the words, and I felt close to a pioneer people I never knew in mortality.

With marriage and college graduation, the fun and excitement of choir faded in the brightness of responsibilities as a husband and father. Music continued in our home, however, whether by the piano, fun little music instruments, the voice, or commercial media. My wife and I both loved music, and wanted its continuing influence in our home.

I thought my performing experiences in music had seen their climax in college, but I was soon to be surprised. I would learn that college days only prefaced what was about to take place.

I was watching a conference broadcast while living in Tempe, Arizona. The Mormon Tabernacle Choir was singing. I was particularly moved at the sound of their voices, and became touched by a feeling of nostalgic anxiety to be closer to them. As I listened with feeling to one of their songs, something inside of me whispered, "Someday you will sing with the Mormon Tabernacle Choir." I was a bit startled, and wondered about the source of the voice. I kept the message inside, not daring to share it with anyone for fear it might have been just a fleeting thought, with no hope for future fulfillment.

Later on in the year, I was surprised with an opportunity to move to West Jordan, Utah, to teach seminary near there. The thought of choir membership came back to memory, for I knew that West Jordan was close to Temple Square. I shared my feelings with my wife, asking if she would like to sing with the choir (but warning her to keep confident my thoughts in case they didn't materialize). Would that opportunity really come to us, I wondered?

We moved during the first of the summer. After settling in our new home in West Jordan, I got a job working in my home town of Orem. Since there was a forty-five-minute drive each day to work and back, I used that time to vocalize and get my voice in shape for a tryout for the Mormon Tabernacle Choir, never having shared my hope and desire with anyone but my wife.

At the close of the summer, I began to doubt the inspiration of such a desire. However, a comment made by a close friend of mine (Neal Adams) who was visiting us in our home, indicated that his brother-in-law (a choir member) had said that there might be some openings for new choir members. The statement came in such a manner as to spark both hope and a commitment to try out.

I later called Richard P. Condie on the phone. My nervousness was greater than that experienced when calling a girl during high school days to ask for a date. (That nervousness was great enough to motivate me to stand outside of the sliding glass doors by the phone, in freezing, snowy weather, so that no one in the family could hear me talking.) When Brother Condie answered, I felt like hanging up and not admitting who I was. Determination welled up, however, and I introduced myself and said that I would like to make an appointment to try out for the Mormon Tabernacle Choir. He informed me that he was busy right then, having just returned from a tour with the choir in Europe. "Call me back in a couple of weeks," he said, and we closed the conversation.

Two weeks later I called and said, "Brother Condie, this is Brent Farley. You told me to call you now to make an appointment for a tryout." We made the appointment and then I asked, "Can I bring my wife with me? She sings too." He informed me that he had no openings in the choir for women. With a determination unusual for me in the audience of a great person, I said, "Well, why don't you just listen to her anyway, and then if the time comes that you do need a sister in the choir, you'll already know what she sounds like."

With a tone that resembled a patient and loving grandfather giving in to a little grandchild asking for candy, he said, "Well, all right. Bring her along."

The appointed day arrived amidst both prayers of hope and fears of failure. We prayed again, then journeyed to Temple Square. On the way we vocalized, hoping our voices would be at their primes.

Entering the lower level of the Assembly Hall, we met Brother Condie himself. This was enough of an experience for me to treasure for life. He welcomed us and led us into his studio.

"Who's first?" he asked.

"I am," I stated. I knew my wife was a natural singer, whereas my talent had come with money for lessons and much hard work. She looked and sounded better than I, so I thought a good finish might help our chances of entering the choir.

I spent perhaps a half an hour with Brother Condie. He tested everything. I felt like I was receiving a voice lesson. When we finished, I took a seat while my wife tried out. He conducted a similar audition with her. My hopes diminished as the time in tryouts increased.

Finally we were through. We sat together facing him. He bowed his head in thought. "We've failed," I thought. Then it occurred to me that perhaps he misunderstood our intentions in trying out. He had spoken to us of his private voice students from time to time, and I wondered if he thought that he had been auditioning us to see if we could become private vocal students.

"We can't pay the cost of the lessons," I thought to myself. "I'd better tell him that we came to try out for the choir, not voice lessons. But then, if I do that, he might think it funny that we thought we could qualify for choir membership. That could be embarrassing."

I was still debating with myself about how best to get out of what was becoming an embarrassing situation when he lifted his head, smiled at us, and said, "We'll be happy to welcome both of you into the Mormon Tabernacle Choir."

That special, secret voice had been true. "Someday you will sing with the Mormon Tabernacle Choir," it had whispered. That "someday" had arrived. Brother Condie told us to report to the choir secretary in two weeks and we would be assigned choir numbers and uniforms. We thanked him, shook hands, and left. Whether or not our feet touched the pavement as we left Temple Square I can't recall.

We soon became immersed in the work and joy of singing with members of the church referred to as "The Lord's Choir." I found that the feelings of music experienced in college days were again heightened. The medium of song became again the medium for prayer and worship in my life as I sang with the baritone section of the Mormon Tabernacle Choir.

I was impressed that television performances always seemed to come off better than the rehearsals. There was a spirit that took over when the camera came on, and the lifting influence of the Lord became apparent.

Many were the joys in singing with the choir. Can you imagine what it is like to stand in the Mormon Tabernacle Choir and sing "The Battle Hymn of the Republic"? Chills and tears combined in that declaration of worship. Singing President Harold B. Lee's favorite song at his funeral in the tabernacle was another unforgettable experience. The choir tours were always exciting, but filled with more work than pleasure, it seemed. Wherever we sang, whatever the circumstances, regardless of the energy level of the members, the Spirit of the Lord was always present, and the power of testimony was raised on the wings of song in a musical witness to the world of the Lord's work.

Brother Condie retired and we sang under the direction of Brother Jay Welch. The, when he left, we sang with Brother Otley. Brother Otley required us to audition again, as well as all of the other members of the choir. Again I went through the nervousness of wondering if I could make it.

Our appointed day arrived. Again we drove toward Temple Square. This time I had a cold that I knew would affect my vocal abilities. I explained the situation to Brother Otley when we arrived, but he told me to go ahead and audition anyway. He could make allowance for the cold and still determine my abilities and vocal quality.

The tryout commenced. I had prayed again in my mind for help. Could I pass?

The hardest part of this audition was on tonal memory. He played several notes on the piano that seemed to have no relationship with each other whatsoever, except that they belonged to keys on the same piano. Then he said, sing that back to me. I started out singing what I thought were the pitches he had played. About two-thirds of the way through, I felt entirely lost and thought to myself, "I've really missed it. Should I just quit where I am?" I decided to continue and guess at what I thought were the remaining notes. Ending somewhere that I thought wasn't especially close to where he ended, I waited for the verdict. He looked up at me and said with surprise, "You're only the second choir member who has been able to sing that back perfectly."

I smiled on the outside, thanked Heavenly Father on the inside. We both made the choir again.

I was impressed with the fact that we always sang a few hymns during our performances. We were never to become so musically "elite" that we couldn't sing a simple, inspiring hymn from the hymnbook. These always tied our performances together, and carried the power of the Spirit.

I thought "this is the church job I'd like to retire in. I'm happy and settled here." But our days with the choir came to an earlier close than I had anticipated. For me, a call to be bishop ended my participation two years after entry. For my wife, the priority of a child was greater than singing with the world's greatest choir, and she soon resigned to the higher call of being a mother at home. With gratitude in our hearts, we turned in our music, and left Temple Square carrying memories and feelings that could never be "checked back in."

King Mosiah longed to sing with such a choir in a different sphere, when he said, "I say unto you that I have caused that ye should assemble yourselves together that I might rid my garments of your blood, at this period of time when I am about to go down to my grave, that I might go down in peace, and my immortal spirit may join the choirs above in singing the praises of a just God." (Mosiah 2:28.)

Perhaps Mormon had the same longing. "And he hath brought to pass the redemption of the world, whereby he that is found guiltless before him at the judgment day hath it given unto him to dwell in the presence of God in his kingdom, to sing ceaseless praises with the choirs above, unto the Father, and unto the Son, and unto the Holy Ghost, which are one God, in a state of happiness which hath no end." (Mormon 7:7.)

Joseph Smith may have had similar feelings as he prayed, "And help us by the power of thy Spirit, that we may mingle our voices with those bright, shining seraphs around thy throne, with acclamations of praise, singing Hosanna to God and the Lamb!" (D&C 109:79.)

There is a divine power for good in music. But there is also a caution. "Wherefore, all things which are good cometh of God; and that which is evil cometh of the devil; for the devil is an enemy unto God, and fighteth against him continually, and inviteth and enticeth to sin, and to do that which is evil continually." (Moroni 7:12.)

There is music that comes from God. There is also music that comes from the devil. Through unclean lyrics, loud distorted sounds and driving beats, Satan entices and invites toward sin. We must be careful to monitor, as much as possible, the music that comes into our homes. Music that is uplifting and clean, whether religious or secular, will lift our spirits, and bring us closer to the Savior. Music which comes from other sources is degrading, and will cause us to sink away from the Savior. The dividing line is real and perceivable. After singing with the Mormon Tabernacle Choir during a rehearsal, I would sometimes unthinkingly turn on the radio to listen to a local FM station that played good music. Even with this mild, secular music, the drop in spirit was so realistic that I switched the radio off, not wanting to lose the height attained during choir rehearsal. If the difference is that obvious between sacred and secular when both are good, how obvious it should be between sacred and evil, good and bad. One cannot listen to the music inspired by Satan and claim to be fully worshipping the Lord with his life. Satan's music is incompatible with the life of a saint. "Even so every good tree bringeth forth good fruit; but a corrupt tree bringeth forth evil fruit.

"A good tree cannot bring forth evil fruit, neither can a corrupt tree bring forth good fruit." (Matthew 7:17-18.)

It is so with music. Music can lift the soul to the heavens, or sink it toward hell.

The Savior and his apostles sung a hymn before going to the Garden of
Gethsemane. What kind of a hymn do you think they sang? Would it have
a parallel in our hymnbook today? What kind of a spirit did they sing with?
What kind of a spirit do you sing with? What kind of music penetrates the
atmosphere of your home?

"For my soul delighteth in the song of the heart; yea, the song of the
righteous is a prayer unto me, and it shall be answered with a blessing upon
their heads." (D&C 24:12.)

CHAPTER FIFTEEN

Saints:
The Embryos Of Gods

When I left for the mission field, it was a difficult thing for me to say goodbye to my parents. The final embrace at the airport was filled with emotion, and something inside of me wanted to stay. Yet something else pulled me toward a distant land to preach the gospel. I knew I wanted to serve as the Lord had called me, and so I left for my mission.

While serving as a missionary, the influence of my home and parents was ever present. I enjoyed my mission immensely, but there was always a hope and desire to be reunited with my parents at the end of my service. The time of my return came, and the thrill of seeing my family waiting for me at the airport is difficult to describe.

So it is with mortality. We left the presence of our Father and Mother in heaven. Perhaps we longed to stay, yet surely desired the experience of mortality. And so we left for our missions in the field of service called "earth." Though away from home, the influence of heavenly parentage and moorings is ever available. Imagine the joy when we return to see Heavenly Father and Mother smiling, waiting to embrace us again and welcome us home. Think of the joy to stand in the presence of the Savior and hear the words "Well done, thou good and faithful servant . . . enter thou into the joy of thy lord." (Matthew 25:21.)

"When the Savior shall appear we shall see him as he is.

"And that same sociality which exists among us here will exist among us there, only it will be coupled with eternal glory, which glory we do not now enjoy." (D&C 130:1-2.)

The opportunity for that glorious reunion is available to all of the saints if they but live for it. But there is more than the joy of reunion available. There is the legacy of inheritance.

We have a divine genealogy. Literal tracing of ancestry would take us back to Adam and Eve. One step further back would lead to God. "And this is the genealogy of the sons of Adam, who was the son of God. . . ." (Moses 6:22.)

Having come from celestial parents, we inherited the potential to become celestial ourselves. No one came from anyone less than perfect beings, for those are the only individuals allowed to have the privilege of having spirit children. We all began equal, with divine potential.

The use of free agency, however, broke up that equality of potential. In the first estate rebellion and war occurred, resulting in the loss of a third part of the host of heaven. (Revelation 12:7-9.) On the other hand, many of Heavenly Father's spirit children became noble and great. (Abraham 3:22-23.)

For those who did not rebel, plans were made for further development, which included a mortal experience upon earth. Through the "fall" of Adam and Eve, we gained the opportunity to depart from our home for a season to live in mortality where we would be tested and tried, experiencing growth and maturity if we followed the heavenly plan of the gospel.

Now, upon earth, we live in a vital stage of existence—most vital. If we fail here, we lose the opportunity for both a joyous reunion and a celestial inheritance. Alma said, "This life is the time for men to prepare to meet God; yea, behold the day of this life is the day for men to perform their labors." (Alma 34:32.)

The Lord revealed that "They who keep their second estate [mortality] shall have glory added upon their heads for ever and ever." (Abraham 3:26.)

As in the premortal experience, free agency separates mortal individuals into classes. One must choose to return home to Heavenly Father. "Therefore . . . whosoever will come may come and partake of the waters of life freely; and whosoever will not come the same is not compelled to come; but in the last day it shall be restored unto him according to his deeds." (Alma 42:27.)

Having chosen correctly, one must follow through with actions by receiving the gospel. The Lord said, "And this is my gospel—repentance and baptism by water, and then cometh the baptism of fire and the Holy Ghost, even the Comforter, which showeth all things, and teacheth the peaceable things of the kingdom." (D&C 39:6.)

These principles and ordinances are available only within one church: The Church of Jesus Christ of Latter-day Saints. Of this church, the Savior revealed that it is ". . . the only true and living church upon the face of the whole earth." (D&C 1:30.) Rejection of membership in His church amounts to rejection of the Lord Himself.

Once within the church, one must progress as a Latter-day Saint as directed by the Spirit of the Lord. "For behold, I say unto you that if ye will enter in by the way, and receive the Holy Ghost, it will show unto you all things what ye should do." (2 Nephi 32:5.)

This progress is attained by degrees, "For he will give unto the faithful line upon line, precept upon precept; and I will try you and prove you herewith." (D&C 98:12.)

Along the pathway of progress comes the reception of the priesthood for faithful brethren. Within this reception of priesthood is the promise from Heavenly Father of divine inheritance:

"For whoso is faithful unto the obtaining these two priesthoods of which I have spoken, and the magnifying their calling, are sanctified by the Spirit unto the renewing of their bodies.

"They become the . . . elect of God.

"And also all they who receive this priesthood receive me, saith the Lord;

"For he that receiveth my servants receiveth me;

"And he that receiveth me receiveth my Father;

"And he that receiveth my Father receiveth my Father's kingdom; therefore all that my Father hath shall be given unto him.

"And this is according to the oath and covenant which belongeth to the priesthood." (D&C 84:33-39.)

Magnification embodies seeing clearly the duties of a saint, and bringing into focus the finer details of gospel living. The key is living so as to be worthy of the guiding inspiration of the Spirit, and so ". . . every one that hearkeneth to the voice of the Spirit cometh unto God, even the Father.

"And the Father teacheth him of the covenant which he has renewed and confirmed upon you." (D&C 84:47-48.)

Thus Paul taught, ". . . Walk in the Spirit, and ye shall not fulfill the lust of the flesh." (Galatians 5:16.)

A spiritual individual is becoming like our Heavenly parents; a non-spiritual person sinks to a state of nature wherein one lives for self-preservation and acts by instinct, as do the animals. Such do not qualify for celestial inheritance.

A man or woman alone cannot reach celestial heights. Paul said, "Nevertheless neither is the man without the woman, neither the woman without the man, in the Lord." (1 Corinthians 11:11.) Each must be converted to and united in the gospel. This conversion and unity will lead to the temple.

"If you would become a son or a daughter of God and an heir of the kingdom, then you must go to the house of the Lord and receive blessings which there can be obtained and which cannot be obtained elsewhere; and you must keep those commandments and those covenants to the end."*

The Lord revealed that "In the celestial glory there are three heavens or degrees;

"And in order to obtain the highest, a man must enter into this order of the priesthood [meaning the new and everlasting covenant of marriage];

"And if he does not, he cannot obtain it.

"He may enter into the other, but that is the end of his kingdom; he cannot have an increase." (D&C 131:4.)

Climbing the gospel ladder must be a constant effort, and stopping short of the top rung fails to bring the greatest blessings. Nephi taught:

"And now, my beloved brethren, after ye have gotten into this straight and narrow path, I would ask if all is done? Behold, I say unto you, Nay; for ye have not come thus far save it were by the word of Christ with unshaken faith in him, relying wholly upon the merits of him who is mighty to save.

"Wherefore, ye must press forward with a steadfastness in Christ, having a perfect brightness of hope, and a love of God and of all men. Wherefore, if ye shall press forward, feasting upon the word of Christ, and endure to the end, behold, thus saith the Father: Ye shall have eternal life." (2 Nephi 31:19-20.)

As one endures and presses on in the gospel, intelligence and joy become byproducts. Joseph Smith stated:

"We consider that God has created man with a mind capable of instruction, and a faculty which may be enlarged in proportion to the heed and diligence given to the light communicated from heaven to the intellect; and that the nearer man approaches perfection, the clearer are his views, and the greater his enjoyments, till he has overcome the evils of his life and lost every desire for sin."†

For such individuals Jesus prayed that the joy he had might be shared with them: "And now come I to thee; and these things I speak in the world, that they might have my joy fulfilled in themselves." (John 17:13.)

Thus, by choosing to accept the Lord and His church, and by progressing from principle to principle and ordinance to ordinance, we secure our inheritance in the highest degree of the celestial kingdom, and attain the joy of the saints. Our first heirship was inherited as the result of our birth as spirit children of divine parentage; the second one is attained and earned by personal worthiness. Of those who so achieve it is said:

"They are they who received the testimony of Jesus, and believed on his name and were baptised after the manner of his burial, being buried in

---

*Joseph Fielding Smith, *Doctrines of Salvation, op. cit.,* Vol. 2, p. 40.
†Joseph Smith, *Teachings of the Prophet Joseph Smith, op. cit.,* p. 51.

the water in his name, and this according to the commandment which he has given—

"That by keeping the commandments they might be washed and cleansed from all their sins, and receive the Holy Spirit by the laying on of the hands of him who is ordained and sealed unto this power;

"And who overcome by faith, and are sealed by the Holy Spirit of promise, which the Father sheds forth upon all those who are just and true." (D&C 76:51-53.)

"These shall dwell in the presence of God and his Christ forever and ever." (D&C 76:62.)

"They shall pass by the angels . . . to their exaltation and glory in all things." (D&C 132:19.)

"Then shall they be gods." (D&C 132:20.)

Years ago I stood outside the garden tomb in Jerusalem. I was a tourist. I wanted to see the spot where the Savior had lain. I waited until the line of tourists had cleared away, then approached the tomb. I stooped to enter, then straightened up inside the tomb. The voice of the Spirit said to me, "He is not here." I had a burning impression that He had risen. He was the Savior. He had triumphed over death, the final enemy, and had entered into His kingdom of glory. His inheritance was attained, and the path was set for the saints to follow.

Every faithful Latter-day Saint may obtain a celestial inheritance by following the steps of the Savior along the pathway of gospel progression. It is my hope that *Spiritually Yours* will be one of the helpful markers along the way.